D0205410

monologues
for women

She Speaks

revised edition

nusa '04

She Speaks

Monologues for Women

revised edition

compiled and edited by Judith Thompson

Playwrights Canada Press
Toronto • Canada

Playwrights Canada Press
The Canadian Drama Publisher
215 Spadina Ave., Suite 230, Toronto, ON, Canada M5T 2C7
phone 416.703.0013 fax 416.408.3402
info@playwrightscanada.com • www.playwrightscanada.com

Playwrights Canada Press acknowledges the financial support of the Government of Canada through the Canada Book Fund and the Canada Council for the Arts, and of the Province of Ontario through the Ontario Arts Council and the Ontario Media Development Corporation, for our publishing activities.

 Canada Council for the Arts **Conseil des Arts du Canada**   **ONTARIO ARTS COUNCIL** **CONSEIL DES ARTS DE L'ONTARIO**

  **Ontario**
Ontario Media Development Corporation

Front cover collage by Nusa Prijatelj
Production Editing/Cover Design: JLArt

Library and Archives Canada Cataloguing in Publication

She speaks : monologues for women / selected and edited by Judith Thompson. -- Rev. ed.

Includes index.
ISBN 978-0-88754-828-4

1. Monologues, Canadian (English) 2. Women--Drama. 3. Acting--Auditions.
4. Canadian drama (English)--20th century. I. Thompson, Judith, 1954-

PS8309.M6S564 2006   C812'.04508054   C2006-900615-6

First revised edition: February 2006. Third printing: June 2011
Printed and bound in Canada by Hignell Book Printing, Winnipeg

This book is dedicated to the memory of Carol Bolt (1941-2000), one of the founders of Playwrights Guild of Canada who spoke out with power and humour and unending love. She continues to speak through all of us.

Table of Contents

Judith Thompson is the author of *The Crackwalker*, *White Biting Dog*, *I Am Yours*, *Lion in the Streets*, *Sled*, *Perfect Pie*, *Habitat*, *Capture Me* and *Enoch Arden*. She has written two feature films "Lost and Delirious" and "Perfect Pie" as well as television movies and radio drama. Her work has enjoyed great success internationally. She is professor of Drama at the University of Guelph and currently lives with her husband and five children in Toronto.

Introduction to *She Speaks: Monologues for Women*
Judith Thompson

*Above all, a monologue must give voice
to those who have been silenced.*

When Angela Rebeiro approached me about editing a book of monologues for women, I agreed without hesitation. The monologue for me is like water to a swimmer, it is the form I began writing more than 25 years ago and it is the form I am happiest writing in; so I dove in and I have been swimming happily, deeply in this book for the last two years.

For someone who thrills to the sound of a unique dramatic "voice" like an anthropologist might thrill to finding a 2000-year-old pot, this process has been endlessly gratifying; I believe that it is only in writing the monologue that the writer discovers the true voice of the character, and more significantly, the dragon that lives underneath the surface life of that character. For me, writing drama has always been about finding the dragon and hearing it roar.

In choosing the monologues for this collection my mandate, in a way, was "is there a dragon in here?"

The dragon, for me, is the unconscious life of the speaker and the monologue is the dragon breathing fire.

The sound of a good monologue is almost as important as the content; it is a kind of lush and smacking music, the language of the soul, language moulded and twisted and carved to express precisely, and perfectly what needs to be expressed. We are enthralled by a powerful monologue in part because we are rarely permitted to indulge in our own monologues, if we do transgress and speak out to our friends or associates for longer than 30 seconds or so, unless we are brilliantly witty, or at a rally for public health care, we will quickly clear the room.

When I wrote my first play, *The Crackwalker*, I gave each of the characters a monologue, framing the play—and they were all audience addresses. "Who are they talking to?" the actors would ask, in frustration. And I could only reply "the audience." I hated the idea of a phony set-up with a social worker, or a psychiatrist, or someone in the "listening" professions—to justify a long monologue; never explain, the monologue is part of a long theatrical tradition, it is direct, it is intimate. And there is no looking away from it, we must go on the journey of the monologue with the character, even if he or she is breathing fire that burns the air we breathe.

The monologues in *She Speaks: Monologues for Women* certainly represent my personal taste in monologues. I like them deeply theatrical, volcanic, raw, deeply funny and utterly unique; I like a certain sound, the delicious and dangerous music of the voice; I like diversity in every aspect of the word, and most of all, I wanted them speakable, in and of the stage; I wanted to give all the brilliant actresses out there some white hot sizzling new and in many cases, untried monologues to use for audition pieces, or to put together an enthralling evening to showcase their versatility and their power.

From Randi Helmers's searing and unforgettable reflection on the night when the speaker's brother committed suicide—"why didn't the dog bark?"—to Sally Clark's laugh-out-loud hilarious upper class eccentric character pieces, to Dionne Brand's West Indian young girl ghost to Djanet Sears's chalk-eating bereaved doctor to Nina Aquino's young Filipina aching for Marilyn blondness to Charlotte Coleman's complicated memories of the summer her mother died to Janice Keefer's prickly and enchanting Katherine Mansfield to Anne Lambert's shame and desire in the Honduras to Tony Berto's small town bouncer to Celia McBride's young lover with bites all over her body to Daniel MacIvor's dream of drowning to Monique Mojica's massacre survivor to Emma Roberts's waitress meeting up with the ruined antiquer to Colleen Wagner's unbearable unearthing; I could go on and on and on, for every one of the monologues in this book has a shattering and healing power, delivered in a unique and unforgettable voice.

The speaker must urgently need to speak, to proclaim, to persuade, to incite, to inspire, to agitate, to fabricate, to contaminate or whitewash, to justify; the speaker needs approval, or absolution, or acclaim, or worship, or laughter or sympathy. The monologue can only happen if the speaker has an audience. The monologue is ultimately the electric interaction between the audience and the speaker.

Write a monologue: Give voice to the silent, and make the invisible visible.

September 2004

she
speaks

ADOLESCENCE

"mary"
from

yagayah
naila belvett and d'bi.young

mary is in kingston, jamaica, summertime in 1993. imogene is in montreal, canada, winter 1993.

mary

mi friend imogene deh a foreign fi di last 2 weeks, one place call montreal. every time mi ask har if dat mean seh she deh close to brooklyn, new york she tell me seh she nuh know. well foreign a foreign an who cyaan guh foreign a bat. me dun know seh mi have one whole heap a family a foreign. mi have family a florida, a atlanta, even a new york. mi have family inna a brooklyn, new york city represent. well di one imogene she a mi best friend, wi been bes friend fi, mek mi si, bout thirteen years, since wi a three years old. wi used to give each odda everything, from ice-cream to blouse and skirt to book an pencil. wi did even go a di same basic school togedda. imogene tell mi dat when she get pon top har feet a foreign she

a sen mi new shoes and clothes and nuff panty an brief. well di brief de a fi mi bredda jacob, him a seven now, just turn seven last week. mi hear she foreign nice enuh. tings free. di street dem pave wid gole. an money grow pon tree basically. yuh tink inna foreign people live inna zinc house, a brick dem live inna like inna di story book dem like hansel and grekkle. people nuh live inna poverty and degradation like we do. all di cussing and fighting, looting an murdering nuh gwaan a foreign. inna jam dung life hard an people wi do anyting fi back bite yuh. inna foreign everybody live inna one white picket fence, wid house, an lan, an cyar, an dog and 2.3 pickney. dem even have washing machine and dryer. dem even have machine fi wash up cup an plate. a laziness dat if yuh ask me. but nobody neva ask.

mi soon gwan a foreign but imogene guh quicker dan mi.

from

The Vic
Leanna Brodie

The Vic is a play with eight women and four storylines, united by a search party looking for traces of a missing woman. It deals with themes of power, cruelty, and responsibility. Cara is a suburban teenager who, throughout the play, is recording an intensely private video diary.

CARA

July the 27th: I'm still seventeen. So last week, right, coming back from Toshiro's, I get off the bus, and it's dark out, and there's this park on the way home? It's not big or anything; and there's not a lot of trees or anything; but there's just not any light. And this park goes straight from the bus to our street, right? And if you don't take it, it's a hundred miles around to get home; and I'm late already; and I get off the bus and all I'm thinking about is getting home before "Dawson's Creek" starts. And then I look around: and I'm halfway through the park. And it's really, really dark. So I'm thinking: "Oh great: why am I here: I'm gonna get dragged into a bush," and I'm looking around and it's just as far back as ahead: so I keep going. Really intense, you know; my hand is inside my purse on my rape alarm and the other hand I make a fist like this with my keys poking through; and I'm listening and checking around like crazy. I mean, at this point, if I'm gonna die, I'm gonna die, right? But I'm not gonna make it easy for him.

    Beat.

So I live: and I turn on the show: but I'm thinking and thinking. Why? Why do I do that? I mean, I know it's a war zone out there, and you only have to mess up once, so why do I keep ending up on the edge every once in a while? Because this wasn't the only time I forget for a minute, or court danger, or whatever. You hold some guy's eyes too long on the bus; you kiss someone you don't know very well maybe, because you feel like it; you get a little wasted at a party with too many people. If it ever happened, it's your fault; nobody believes all you wanted was a look or a kiss or a beer; nobody cares what you wanted; whatever. Anyway, I started thinking: what if "zoning out" or pushing the limit or whatever is only a symptom: what's the real reason? And I never figure it out: but I do narrow it down to five. Five Reasons I Get Into Situations Where I Might Possibly Get Assaulted Or Killed. One.

Holds up fist; extends first finger.

Stupidity. Like, the world couldn't exist without me, so I'm going to live forever. I'm cute, I'm nice, I have long, straight hair: who could possibly want to hurt me? Two.

Holds up two fingers.

Ancestor worship. That's not a joke. It makes more sense than God: at least you know your ancestors USED to exist. Maybe I think that, somehow, Grandpa will protect me. Why not? He always did. Three.

Holds up three fingers.

Buffy Syndrome. I took Wendo. I watch "Xena." I'm waiting for someone to start something so I can try out my awesome new moves. This theory might include the Dirty Harriet Factor: with all the scumbags around, I'm mad as hell, and I'm waiting for some punk to make my day. Four.

Holds up four fingers.

So here's where it starts to get weird. Maybe, in the end, if I was really stuck and he was really going to…. Maybe I know in my heart that I would rather die than let him do that to me. And if I got the chance, I'd rather kill him than either. And somehow, that makes me feel stronger.

Silence.

Right: five.

Holds up fingers and thumb.

Five is that I want it to happen. I hate all this pussy-footing around. I hate being a virgin and sometimes I hate my life, but I'm too shy to ask for what I want, so deep down I would like some guy to take me over, and take away the responsibility, and subconsciously I'm putting out the signals until some guy is man enough to just take charge.

Beat. Laughs. Stops. Looks at hand, then at audience. Puts thumb down.

"Sensory Recall"
from

Provenance
Ronnie Burkett

PITY

I discovered the boy in the painting when I was thirteen. A pivotal age, a seminal time, an instance that has influenced the entire life of Pity Beane. He lived in a book—*Trends in 20ʰ Century Art*—forgotten in the school library, and I was only too happy to have him there. He was safe and untouched by others. The art section of my school library was a total no-man's-land, small and tucked away, better still for me, so no one could see as I kissed him, day after day after day. And so it was for three years. Secret and perfect and ours.

As I matured and turned sixteen, I felt that I did not know my boy in the painting as well as I should. I knew a smell to assign to him, but it was musty and somewhat weak, like the pages of the book in which he lived. If I was going to carry him with me, I would have to find a way to marry all my senses to this angelic boy, not just my mind's eye. So, to liberate him from that tomb-like tome, I decided to create a fragrance and a whisper all his own.

I would pretend to be looking in another direction, intentionally brushing up against boys in the hall, or walking right into their chests. And before they would push me aside, or worse, just ignore me, I would inhale. I would take them into my lungs and know their scent. The jock gods reeking of soap and Dentyne, the slackers oozing of tobacco and booze-stained T-shirts. Asian boys wafting through the halls in a haze of ginger and hair gel, christian kids, like salt and vinegar chips, brainiacs and geeks who always smelled like fast food litter left in the back seat of a car. And once, by mistake, a teacher. Mr. Van Ryn, tart and familiar like mayonnaise. But the best were the Italian boys in their rayon shirts, smelling sweet and sweaty like sausages hung in the sun to dry. My beautiful boy in the painting could not have smelled like that, but when I morphed them together in my head, I thought that I would die.

His voice, of course, was another matter. And although in my fantasy we rarely spoke—we didn't need to, you see, we simply understood everything —still, once in a while he would want to tell me how beautiful I was or how much he loved me. So, hello, I needed to hear him. But the problem with modern culture is that every sound has a visual. And I already had the picture. No, hearing my boy was not easy, or perhaps he had nothing to say. And just as I was about to give up, there was a miracle. There was a school play.

See, my high school had this drama teacher, Mr. Garfinkel, who apparently had studied at a lesser institution of higher learning in a suburb of Toronto and that made him like this total theatre expert. He was always doing collectives and student-created work. That's a step up from musicals and murder mysteries I suppose, but, just the same, they were always so lame. But in his mind they were completely relevant to our teenage angst.

Anyway, there was a play—or rather, a student collective—called *Beautiful Voices*, a hodge-podge of melting-pot stories reflecting the diversity of teenage experience and the one-ness of our global village, blah blah blah. It was a series of monologues and choral chanting with yoga-based movement, and featured the usual cast of characters. Amy Tamblidge, this totally annoying born again "ho" with giant tits talking about her dreams for global peace, Randall Betrick ranting on about his parents' divorce, again, Trey Fergusson and Amber Witherspoon in this embarrassing dialogue regarding teenage suicide without having the courtesy to actually perform it for us, Blaine Harker confessing that he was gay—oh puh-leese, like that was news—and now we were all supposed to like him even though he was just as annoying as before but out, and on and on and on, blah blah blah. But near the end, there he was. My miracle. A boy who had never dipped his toe into the cesspool of drama club before, but had been coerced into the group by Mr. Garfinkel because of his brooding intensity and sullen mystique. Which meant he was totally hot, in that damaged and dangerous kind of way.

The boy's name was Angelo Bajrektarevic. He was the son of Yugoslavian immigrants, and although he had been in school as long as I could remember, no one seemed to know him. I stood next to him once on the football field during a weekly bomb threat, and he smelled divine.

Like cheese. Not wholesome and annoying like cheddar, or stinky like Stilton, no, kind of foreign and funky, like Camembert wrapped in cashmere. I'll admit I had a bit of a crush on him, but I was already committed, I was totally seeing someone, hello, I was practically engaged to the boy in the painting. And besides, like Uncle Boyfriend always said, fantasizing about someone real only leads to disappointment.

I have no idea why I went to see *Beautiful Voices*, but I'm glad I did. Because somewhere near the end, after all the whining drama club assholes had tortured us all night, Angelo Bajrektarevic came out into a pool of light, set his gaze beyond the audience and spoke. Of loss, of grief, of the sadness that he would never know the homeland his parents had fled. And why? For what? Invisible lines, that's why people bled. Erecting borders between brothers where none had been before. Drawing lines in the sand, that's what men call war. And as he finished, his eyes levelled with ours— no, with mine—and he stared out and simply, softly, surely said, "This school is full of stupid assholes. Nothing is beautiful, but you only know that when you're dead." And then he took a gun out of his jacket and pointed it at the audience. No, pointed it at me, like he was going to shoot me through the heart with his truth. And laughed, like a mad angel, cast out from Heaven. I don't know if that was the end of the play or not, because everyone started screaming and rushing for the exits. But I sat there, frozen. Fuck that was a good play.

Rumour was that Mr. Garfinkel actually shit himself backstage. Angelo, of course, was expelled, and he never came back to school. I think about him though, and hope he's okay. He's going to have a hard life, because he figured things out far too soon and that's no way to get along. But I wish I could have told him that part of what he said was wrong. There is beauty in the world. You just have to know how to make it up. 'Cause, when I close my eyes and dream of the angelic painted youth whispering in my ear, it's always and forever Angelo's voice I hear.

from

The Monkeyhouse
Ryan Hughes

Crystal (seventeen years old) tells us how ballet prepared her for life, and for her friendship with Angie.

CRYSTAL

I think it's a question of how much can you take. Like in ballet. I was in ballet for like eight years. And the teacher was this old, old woman who couldn't even dance, her spine was all twisted out of whack, like this.

She contorts herself briefly.

I guess she used to be beautiful, and she was *this close* to being famous, and some disorder or something started messing with her spine and it twisted her all around and made her useless. Useless was *her* word. She said if I was gonna be useless, to get out of her class, because she hated all useless people, including herself, that the Useless are what the Useful feed their dogs for treats. She wouldn't call us ballerinas, we were just "girls." When I was seven she screamed in my face,

Contorts again.

"You are not a *real ballerina* until you bleed through your pointe shoes!" And pointe shoes are *so* hard to bleed through. But I tried. I walked around at home on pointe. I scraped, grinded my toes into the stiff old carpet in the basement for half an hour before class. I cried, I was in pain, for months. One class I was gasping and sweating and I couldn't hear the piano for the pain, and she was still *screaming* at me, my toes were sticky in my shoes, I could feel them, but not *enough* because the *screaming*, still, so when she looked away I *kicked* my *toes* into the FLOOR! And I was down, screaming into the floor, they dragged me into a corner, and the shoes were coming off, sliding away from my toes, I couldn't stop screaming, *it hurt so MUCH!* And she was over me and she was smiling! She! Smiling! I was looking up at everyone looking down at me and she held up the bloody shoes and she said, "We have a BALLERINA!"

> *A moment of suspension. She smiles, in great pain, and the memory fades. Pause.*

I don't dance anymore. That moment went away, and it never came back. When I was twelve I met Angie and ballet didn't seem as important, so I quit. Angie is more challenging. It's that moment again and again with Angie. That moment forever. You just take it all, and bleed through your shoes, and smile. I should have quit sooner. Ballet, I mean.

from

The Shape of a Girl
Joan MacLeod

Braidie goes back in time, she is twelve years old.

BRAIDIE

Sofie walks like a cripple, little quarters of blood on her heel, soaking into her white socks. Sofie wears her runners too small because her feet are too big. She is accused of watching the girls get undressed in gym. But I watch too. I want to see who else has hair under their arms or who has thighs as big as mine. I talk to her after volleyball. I told her, I did the best I could.

—**Sofie don't go on the field trip.** See—I said it, in plain English.

—**Why?**

—**Just don't.**

—**But we have to write an essay.**

This is pure Sofie, putting homework ahead of life or death. I tell you—she's an extremely exasperating person. We are all going to see *Hamlet* for the field trip, at a theatre in town. It's not the real *Hamlet*; it's a phony version for kids.

For Emergency Only—*Sortie du secours*. I have studied that sign ever since I can remember. It is written over top of some windows in the bus. I sit three rows down from Sofie. Jackie and Adrienne are behind me.

Sofie is sitting with Lorna. Lorna's dad owns the store on our island; sometimes she works there. We don't know Lorna. We don't even think of Lorna as an actual person.

The ocean shrinks and glitters as we head over the Lions Gate. You can see where we live, lying out there in the strait, all wrapped up in mist. It looks uninhabited, prehistoric. Adrienne and Lorna have switched places. Adrienne is whispering something to Sofie. Sofie is looking dead ahead. Adrienne leans into Sofie so that Sofie is squished up against the side. Sofie's face turns grey.

For Emergency Only. Sofie pushes the window on the bus. It fans out unnaturally from the bottom. Sofie hoists herself up, her head is out. Sofie is going to jump out the window. The ocean is hundreds of feet below.

I shut my eyes. And Sofie is falling, cannonballing over the side of the bridge, her clothes parachute around her, a gigantic flower. I open my eyes. Sofie hasn't gone over the side of anything. Her bum is stuck in the window of the bus.

Amber and Adrienne and me and Jackie—we laugh so hard we nearly puke. Sofie is all weird and breathing heavy. Then she pushes out a sound that is hardly human. **Ha-ha.**

The bus driver is grabbing Sofie by the sweater. He pulls her in. **What the hell do you think you're doing?** Adrienne watches Sofie. **Nothing,** Sofie says. **Fooling around.**

Sofie isn't allowed to see the play. We watch Ophelia load herself up with flowers and sail off to meet her maker. We make burp noises except when Hamlet's around. Hamlet's cute.

When Hamlet gets going on one of his long speeches we go **oh oh oh oh** like we are Hamlet's own girlfriend. Then this lady usher comes and tells us we have to be quiet. She's a total bitch.

"Emily" by Emily Sugerman
from

The End of Pretending
Emily Sugerman and Charlotte Corbeil-Coleman

Emily, fifteen years old, is staying with Charlotte and her parents. She is in a constant state of confusion through the events of the summer. Boys, drinking, and Charlotte's constant denial about her mother's dying, leave her contemplative on what it means to grow up. This is Emily's last monologue in the play.

EMILY

I can't remember anything. No specific events, no conversations, no details, which rather puts a damper on trying to think about the past. The only way I can recall time is to hear a song or smell a smell I can associate with a feeling. Then, suddenly, waves of that feeling smash into my stomach. Lou Reed recalls *Wuthering Heights* and Body Shop hand lotion and feeling so so so scared and vulnerable and masochistically emotional. And then, suddenly, memories flitter by and I remember them in slight shock and then I forget them again and only retain the knowledge that I recently wanted to read about Heathcliff and Catherine. But it's too hard to know about my life, too hard for my body, so it blocks out pain or at least dulls it so I can't remember, I can't remember, I can't remember anything. And I place strange baggage on seemingly unrelated subjects such as my inexplicable hatred for Alan Rickman. I hate Alan Rickman. I hate coriander. I hate being an emotional basket case. *(pause)* I remember lying on my bed weeping for my life, drowning in mucous and wiping my runny nose on my pajamas. Staring at my ceiling, bargaining with God, and eating rose petals in confusion. Stepping on people's shoes and staring at their necks and never once escaping into other worlds like all those mothers and fathers and movies and teachers thought we would.

from

I, Claudia
Kristen Thomson

Claudia is an official pre-teen, still reeling from her parents' divorce. Finding refuge in the basement of her school, through the play Claudia discovers the pain at the centre of her brimming child's heart.

CLAUDIA

Some kids are mad when they're teenagers, right? Like in movies and at school lots of kids hate their dads. For different reasons at different times. Some kids hate their dads 'cause they want to shoot speed into their arms! Dads don't let them. Dads try to stop them. They say "Fuck off, Dad. Fuck off! I'm shooting speed into my arm and you can't stop me!" And that's 'cause they're into speed.

But I would *never* do that 'cause I don't hate my dad. My dad is my best friend and I get to see him every week! It starts Monday after school at 3:45. I wait for him in the park across the street from the school and he is never late like other kids' parents and we do something totally bohemian together like go bowling or for pizza. And I have to say, it is the best moment of my entire life because there's so much to talk about and we're both hi-larious. Like every time I say, "I'm thirsty," he says, "I'm Friday," which is just something between us, like father-daughter. And then we go down to his apartment which is a downtown condo where I have my own room with a name plate on the door that says "Albert" for a joke and so I say to him, I say, "al-BERT"—and I have lots of posters, no pets, and I do homework and we just hang out and then I go to sleep. And when I wake up on Tuesday morning it is the worst day of my entire life because it's the beginning of the whole next week of not seeing him. So I come down here on Tuesday morning before class to get control of myself.

But Tuesday is also sophisticated because my Dad leaves for work before me so I get about twenty minutes in the apartment all by myself, which is

a very special time for me which I think of as my teen tim
juice but I drink it out of a coffee mug. I look out over the
and listen to the top music of my time and, um, okay. Mo:
that I do. I take one of my dad's socks from a pair and pac.. .. ..,
like a juice box, pudding cup, whatever. I just do it for a joke-game to see
if he notices that something is missing…. And then I put hair from my
mother's brush under my dad's pillow to help them get along. I learned
that in voodoo class. And then I… um… well… kind of, um… sneak
around to find out information. And there is a lot of information. Look
what I found out for example six months ago! These! *(high heels)* I went to
my dad next time like, "look what I found by accident. What's? Like whose
are these?" And he goes like, fake normal, "Oh those belong to Leslie."

I'm like "WHO?"

"Leslie is a special friend of mine."

Now, I don't want to sound precocious, but I know a euphemism when
I hear one. And then, when I finally saw her I KNEW from her boobs how
special she was. They were like two flying saucers from another planet that
came down and landed on her chest! She came walking into my dad's
apartment on a MONDAY night all globbed over in nail polish and lipstick
and perfume AND wearing a mink coat with no care for the animals and
high heels six feet off the ground! Which are bondage! They are bondage
for women! You can get very, you can get very good supportive shoes.
My grandmother died from osteoporosis and the bones in her feet like
crumbled, they fell apart, and they had big knobs on them so she couldn't
even hardly walk and she told me that it was from wearing high heels. So,
I'm only twelve-and-three quarters and I already know that. And so Leslie
is not very… um… not very… Leslie is… like… stupid…. She says,
"Kiddo." She says, "let's you and me be such good friends, and just do girl
stuff together, stuff your dad can't do 'cause he's a guy, and we can be such
good girlfriends and you can tell me all your problems…"

And I'm like, "Think about it Leslie."

Like, that's just one example of her brain.

"Blandy's Story"
Judith Thompson

BLANDY

Okay like I'm peeing myself laughin in the hall okay? With my girls? We're like "Yo, what up, mami" "nothin much, what up wich you, girl?" we are at Crystal's locker, decorating it crazy for her fourteenth birthday, even though I heard she was talkin shit about me and I said to her "I don't talk shit about you why you talk shit about me?" and I was gonna show her I don't talk shit by doin up her locker with condoms and cigarettes and that and Perez he walks up and I am like OH MY GOD because decorating lockers is automatic suspension, eh, so I'm like passing out and he's like: "Blandy, I wanna talk to you" I go "what, I'm not doing nothing, asshole, are you serious? what do you think I have a weapon? Do I look like I would carry a weapon?" and Serelle goes "Dry" he goes "no I'm not pissed off at you even though you got zero on your all about me skit because you didn't prepare nothing" well so what I didn't prepare my mother took me to Casino Niagara for two days because last time she left me home the neighbour called the Children's Aid and they took me to a foster home he sez "BLANDY I want you to be the star in the play for class." I'm like "what play. A play? That's so gay," He's like "don't say that, and it's *Hamlet*. I'm like "what. you gotta be kidding me I never been in a play since grade one" he's like "you're in it." I'm like "okay okay but I don't want to look bad whose doin the costumes?" he's like "Cooper." I'm like "COOPER? The pool teacher?" We all hate him we hate gettin into our bathing suits for pool because he is lookin at our butts, his eyes when he is lookin at us reminds me of the look on a dog's eyes when he is eating his own vomit? so all the girls every single one of us have their period every time it's pool, there is like one nerdy girl in the pool. We don't want him lookin at our butts not because they are big, though, nobody I know worries about havin a big butt I mean yeah, we worry about it, but you gotta be really fat to be called fat in my school. And nobody wants to be blonde, in fact if you are blonde? You dye your hair brown.

So I'm like "I'm not doin it if Cooper is doin the costumes" so Perez is like "so you do your own costume" and I'm like "YES. Cause I don't care what part I am playin I am wearing my sweatpants and my hoodie and my hair in a ponytail and really good shoes."

So I go "okay I'm doin it what part?" he's like "Hamlet. There's gonna be three Hamlets and two of them are girls." So I go "everyone's gonna be girls, you're not gonna get any boys to do the play, sir, because if you say play the boys will say no fuckin way a play? that's so gay" if you are a boy you are a baller or a skater and nothin in between. He's like "I got the boys already. They have to do it it's for class" and he gives me the script. I'm like "you don't expect me to actually read this thing do you?" And he goes "I'll show you the movie but you gotta try readin it." So I take it home and I do try to read it but I can't understand nothing. I throw it against the wall. Next day I'm like: "I'm not doin it I have my period" he goes "okay okay forget the script here is what you gotta say" and he has it all like down. He says "BLANDY listen and spit out your gum since you are Hamlet three your first line is 'Mother? Mother?' Now mother what's the matter you ever said that? Huh? Huh? Huh?" and he is in my face I'm like "Okay, okay, yah, only every fucking day with my mother" because my mother, Theresa? she is always crying, almost like she's not a mother, like she's a kid like she is mental… And I am like really pissed off at her for gettin with this shithead and she thinks I'm gonna kill her she goes help wilt thou kill me and fuck I'm hearin that thinkin this is just like when my mom called the cops on me just because I pulled a knife on her well she was callin me a slut I'm like thirteen so she says to the cops my daughter is trying to kill me lyin bitch so I am startin to like get it good get it down and when I kill that little mouth Polonius it's like I'm killin someone who I'm not sayin who it is and I go thou finds to be too busy is some danger and I'm like oh my God it's like I'm talkin to myself because I like to talk, eh, I am BUSY and I am always getting myself into trouble for telling people's secrets it's like I can't help it and so I get in big trouble lots of people don't like me for that AND they say I'm a liar. And then, then I see the ghost of my father and like I see him and my mother she don't see him and that is like when it rains really hard? And I can't sleep and suddenly there is this funny smell in the room? And I look up and there's my grandmother, man, just sittin on my bed playin cards my mother she don't believe me but I can smell her and she is just there, playin cards with herself and she looks at me and she says "go to church" or "don't get pregnant" but Hamlet's father he says "do not forget" but it's the same thing right... And when everything is like goin bad for him? So he goes "fuck me" how all occasions do inform against me. From this time forth, my thoughts be BLOODY or be nothing worth and like I have said that very same thing after Rochelle and them said they were gonna kill me because they thought I liked her boyfriend Shamal who goes to Oakwood they said they were gonna get Kayla's dad's machete? And and I never never said I liked him I wouldn't say that, we was at the Dufferin Mall? In the Food court? and he asked me if I would give him head and I said no way not ever but I told Laura? the one who got her eyebrows burned off? and she told Rochelle and them so they were gonna kill me and they have killed people before that's what my cousin said although he might be lying so I said to myself "my thoughts be bloody or be nothing worth" and when she went to slap me I slapped her first. Left a hand mark on her face for three days.

And this lady? Maureen? She is a professional sword fighter man and they brought her in to teach us the fencing? And I rocked at that, man, I fuckin shined even the lady said and if that tip hadn't be poisoned I woulda beat him man I was all over it right with the swords makin sounds in the air and then how he kills the bad king like "TAKE THIS YOU FUCKER you fucking fucker." They put me in learning centre because school is so boring I don't learn it right? So I am in with people who can't speak English or who are dumb like me but I'm gonna tell you something I got this one part perfect I want you to listen to it, I got it perfect, and I know what it means, too. I got it down so back story first: I used to go to this so-called fako psychic down the street? My mom and I would go to like find out what is gonna happen, and what we should do and she was gettin all this money from my mom and my mom was afraid of her and this bitch was threatening her, right? So I went in and I said this from the play I said:

"Listen you phony bitch this whole thing is shit all you do is talk shit we are not payin you another cent and we are not listening to your shit we defy augury augury okay there is special providence in the fall of a sparrow. IF IT BE NOT NOW TIS NOT TO COME IT IT BE NOT TO COME It will be now if it be not now Yet it will come the readiness is all. THE READINESS IS ALL." I stay up nights sayin this one out loud because I get it, right I get that one more than any of the other lines the readiness is all it's my story, Blandy's story to the end, right? The end was eerie, man my guy, Hamlet he is like keelin over, dying but talking, talking like this guy I seen at that strip mall last year? after the car came up and just shot him like eight times and I am in the hair salon with my mother I come out he is lyin there bleeding and talkin talkin and that is Hamlet, me, makin up with his girlfriend's brother, and then, he is takin his last breath? And he is thinkin, like thinkin of the rest of time, without him talkin, and that is me, imagining like the world without me talkin, without Blandy talkin shit and I almost can't but when I do? It is scary man, a scary place, so quiet a world without Blandy talkin: yeah: the rest… is silence.

"Pink"

Judith Thompson

LUCY, a ten-year-old white girl talking to her dead Black nurse, Nellie, shot in a march, in her open coffin.

LUCY

NELLIE NELLIE NELLIE NELLIE NELLIE NELLIE NELLIE NELLIE NELLIE NELLIE NELLIE NELLIE NELLIE NELLIE NELLIE NELLIE.

NELLIE NELLIE NELLIE NELLIE NELLIE NELLIE NELLIE I want you to come back, to shampoo my hair and make a pink cake and we can sit in the back and roll mealie pap in our hands see, I told you not to go in those marches, and I told you that what you people don't understand, what you didn't see, is apartheid's for YOU. IT'S FOR YOUR PEOPLE'S FEELINGS, see, like we got separate washrooms cause you like to spit, and if we said, "Eww yucch, don't spit," it would hurt your feelings and we got separate movies, cause you like to talk back to movie stars and say "amen" and "that's the way" and that drives us crazy so we might tell you you stink and the only thing I don't get is how come you get paid less for the same job my Mummy says it's because you people don't like money anyway, you don't like TVs and stereos and all that stuff cause what you really like to do is sing and dance. And you don't need money to sing and dance I just… I don't understand why you weren't happy with us, Mummy let you eat as much sugar as you wanted, and we never said anything to you, some days, Mummy says it was up to a quarter-pound, but we know Blacks like sugar so we didn't mind, and we even let you take a silver spoon, I heard Mummy say to her friends, "there goes another silver spoon to Soweto" but she never called the police… and you had your own little room back there, and we even let your husband come once in a while, and that's against the law, Mummy and Daddy could have gone to jail for that, so how come you weren't grateful? How come you stopped singing those Zulu songs in the morning, those pretty songs like that one that was about love and kissing, you stopped singing, and you stopped shampooing my hair, you said I could do it myself, and and your eyes, your eyes used to look at me when I was little they would look at me like they were tickling me just tickling me all the time, like I was special, but they went out, they went out like a light does and you stopped making my cakes every Tuesday, every Tuesday I would ask you to make a pink cake and you would always say, "you ask your mummy" and then you'd make it, but you stopped making them, you told me I was too old for pink cakes, that the pink wasn't real, it was just food colour anyway and then, and then you hardly ever came anymore, and when I saw you that day… when I saw you downtown with your husband and four children all… hanging off your arms, I just couldn't stand it! I wanted to yell at your children and tell them you were mine that you were more mine than theirs because you were with me more much more so you were mine and to let go of you to get off you and I hated the way you looked without your uniform, so brown and plain, not neat and nice anymore, you looked so pretty in your uniform, so pretty, but we didn't even mind when you didn't want to wear it.

We didn't mind, but you were still unhappy, and when I saw you in town looking so dusty and you didn't even introduce me to your kids and one of them, one of them did that rude thing that "Amandilia" thing that means Black power I saw you slap his hand but you didn't say anything, so you must have hated me too, I saw that you hated me too and I'd been so nice to you, I told you my nightmares and you changed my bed when I wet it and now you didn't even like me and it wasn't my fault it wasn't my fault it's just when I asked you why that day, you were cleaning the stove and I said Nellie why… don't you like me anymore, and you said, "you're not a child anymore, Lucy, you're a white person now" and it wasn't my fault and I couldn't help it I couldn't help yelling

KAFFIR, KAFFIR, DO WHAT YOU'RE TOLD, KAFFIR OR I SLAP YOUR BLACK FACE, I SLAP YOUR BLACK FACE AND I KICK YOUR BLACK BELLY I KICK YOUR BLACK BELLY AND KICK IT TILL IT CAVES RIGHT IN AND IT CAN'T HOLD MORE BLACK BABIES EVER AGAIN. NO MORE UGLY BLACK BABIES THAT YOU'LL… that you'll like more than me. Even though I'm ten years old I made you die. I made you go into that march and I made you die. I know that forever. I said I was sorry, I'm sorry, I'm sorry, I'm sorry, I'm sorry, but you never looked at me again. You hated me. But I love you, Nellie, more than Mummy or Daddy and I want you to come back, and sing those songs, and roll mealie pap and be washing the floor in your nice uniform so I can come in and ask you to make a pink cake and your eyes will tickle me. And you will say "yes."

"Yes, I'll make a pink cake…"

"Yearbook Committee"
from

Fables

Jackie Torrens

Fables is about four people desperate for connection: a middle-aged man suffering from depression, a woman encased in a body of multiple cosmetic surgeries, a young man fearful of his physical environment, and a fifteen-year-old girl who is isolated with the secret of a rape and the notion that biology is not her friend. Much of the play is told through monologues. The character in these two monologues, Lisa, is the fifteen-year-old girl.

LISA

When I die? I wanna be cremated. Cause the thought of all those maggots and worms and stuff going in and outta your eye sockets is gross. And I wanna be scattered too, my ashes, I mean. Like what they did to John D after he died playing chicken on the highway. Got hit then dragged five hundred feet under the car. And when they got him out from under there wasn't any blood either. Not one drop. It was all internal bleeding. He was bruised though. Purple. Made me think of a plum. Then they cremated him. That's the way to do it, for sure.

I use ta have panic attacks and stuff cause I started thinking one day, when I die? People might not know I wanna be cremated and it takes a long time for the worms to get through all your flesh. Just the thought of it drives me crazy. So I put up a sign on my dresser that says "cremation"—just so when I die and people are clearing up my stuff they'll look at that sign and go, "oh yeah, Lisa wanted to be cremated." Just like a post-it-note, you know? A memory jogger. Wanna know something funny? My mother's never said anything about it, I don't think she even noticed.

The best part about death is this, there's no "if," just "when." Like, I'm on the yearbook committee, right? Cause I gotta be. Cause everyone else is thinking like, how many pages are we gonna leave for pictures of the hockey team or, how many pages do we leave for whatever rich bitch is gonna be Winter Queen this year, right? But I'm always thinking this—how many blank pages are we gonna leave at the end of the book? How many blank pages, right? No one else wants to think about that, just me. But we gotta, cause ya need a certain number of pages at the back of the book for the dead kids—ya know, the drunk-driving dead kids or the guy that overdoses on mushrooms or whatever. Cause it's gonna happen. It's a good rule of thumb to leave two pages for the prom night car accidents and one for the drug overdose. Then you take their class picture and print the lyrics from their favourite song and maybe you think how you used to see them in the hall all the time and how maybe every so often you said hi to them... the page *remembers* them. That's not morbid, that's realistic.

You always gotta leave one extra page. One extra. Cause there's always the kid who kills themselves. I make sure they get the last page, cause that's the most important one. Like last year, Stevie F? Shot himself in the head, that was a good one. I gave him a beautiful page. Everybody talked after how they knew it was gonna happen and how they were like, best friends with him and so on. I mean, *everyone*. And his funeral—jam-packed, the whole school was there. The Tracies, bawling their heads off, front and centre. Like they ever gave him the time of day. Death makes you popular though. If Stevie was still alive he'd be Winter King this year for sure.

For my funeral? I'm gonna leave *exact instructions*. Like, I want people to play my favourite song, no crappy hymns or nothing. And I'm gonna have a guest list too, so only people I want to be there will be there—no crashers, no phonies. Swear to God, I will rise from the dead if even *one* of the Tracies tries to get in. And I'm gonna write a letter and someone can read it and it's gonna name *names*. Like, who exactly drove me to it. That would be hilarious! So.

I'm on the yearbook committee every year.

Cause someone's gotta remember to leave the extra page.

"Ugly"
from

Fables
Jackie Torrens

Spotlight on Lisa. She is very controlled.

— ◎ — ◎ —

LISA

Maybe this is it. Maybe this is why. There's this girl. At my school. She sits every day at the front of the class, right between the girl with the flat nose and the tall girl with the heart murmur. They're all dogs but SHE is UGLY. She's the worst.

This ugly girl, she's so stupid she thinks if she prays hard enough she'll be invisible. But it never happens. She's too ugly not to be seen. Every day she walks down the hallway at school where the guys line up to look at who goes by. She thinks, *please don't say anything please don't say anything please don't see me.* But they do. They bark. Spit. Make puking sounds.

One day the Ugly Girl meets this guy. A man. He shaves, he's got grease in his fingernails, his tongue tastes like smoke and pepperoni when he kisses her. First time they kiss he puts his hand on her breast and, for the next two days, she imagines it over and over. She can't hear the noise around her at school or at home, that hand on her breast is the only sound she can hear. They do that for a couple of weeks. Meet in his car, hand on her breast, his thing pressed against her leg. I love you so much, he says. I love you too, she says. So *much.* He goes, *c'mon c'mon.* She goes, *not yet.* But one night? At the cemetery? She goes, *oh-kay.* And that's the night he touches her tattoo, so soft. The moth.

Next night? The Man and the Ugly Girl go driving. Get burgers. Pick up one of his friends, drive around some more. Park the car, pass a bottle around. They tell her she's got sexy legs. She likes that. They tell her she's got great tits. She likes that too. The Friend of the Man keeps putting his arm around her and saying things like, what's a gorgeous girl like you doing with this loser! And the Man keeps saying, take your hand off my woman! And they all laugh. Ugly Girl feels so pretty she could burst. So she brags. She brags she loves sex so much she can't get enough. They laugh, they like this talking about sex stuff. Well then, says the Man, and he points down there, try this one for size then. Yeah, says the Friend of the Man, I got something you can suck on. And maybe the Ugly Girl doesn't like this too much. Maybe she's thinking about going home—but now the two men are calling her *cocktease cocktease* and talking about their balls going blue. And now they're laughing again but this time it sounds like the ugliest sound in the world, it sounds like biting teeth, it sounds like wolves. And now maybe they're tugging at her, grabbing her, pulling her top off, pushing her jeans down. *C'mon! c'mon!* they're saying to her. And maybe they get her outta the car, push her on the grass. And the Man goes inside her and the Friend of the Man goes in her mouth. And afterwards she's lying on the grass and she can hear the two men talking about how ugly girls will do it cause they're desperate for attention.

she
speaks

BODY

"Edna Rural"
from

Street of Blood
Ronnie Burkett

EDNA

I've been awake all night. Two Neo Citrans and I still couldn't
sleep. Maybe it was the late show that did it. They were showing that old
Esmé Massengill movie, "Passport to Love." It was one of my favourites.
Esmé played Dixie Carlyle, a waitress in a roadside diner who changes
a flat tire for a travelling foreign prince and falls in love. Oh, so romantic.
But that was our Esmé. Living, breathing passion!

Too bad poor Dixie Carlyle tripped on the train of her dress and got hit
by a speeding taxi as she crossed the street to the church. But she died
beautifully, and oh, I loved that dress! More than anything I had ever seen.
So when my Stanley asked me to help run the farm—which was his idea of
a marriage proposal—I just knew that my wedding dress had to be like the
one in "Passport to Love."

I saw that movie three times down at the old Bijoux, trying to doodle the
dress in the dark. I clipped every picture I could find of it from the movie
magazines. I worked extra hours at Turner's Drugstore during the week,
just so I could save enough money to buy five yards of satin and two of lace
from the catalogue, shipped all the way from Toronto.

I made my pattern from old newspapers, then I cut it out of sugar sacks,
like I use for my quilting, as a kind of test run. Then I scrubbed down the
kitchen table, laid out my precious cloth, and cut. Lord love a duck, I had
never been so nervous in my whole life. It took me weeks to sew that dress,
because I knew that fancy clothes in France were all hand sewn. And since
necessity is the mother of invention, I stained the lace veil pink by dipping
it in a bucket of diluted Saskatoons I'd put through the sieve.

I knew I was no Esmé Massengill, and even though I st... week before the wedding, I was still just lumpy Edna. B... that dress, well, didn't I just feel like a princess.

It was a small wedding and I had only one gal stand up with me, not a tribe of bridesmaids like Esmé. There was no money for that, and besides, I didn't have that many friends.

But Cora Jean Pickles, who worked with me at the drugstore, agreed to be my bridesmaid and matron of honour combined. Cora Jean was saving up her money to go to Winnipeg to study the ballet. It was Cora Jean who gave me the beads for my veil. Took them right off one of her dance recital dresses. I was indebted to her for life because of that.

I don't remember much about my wedding day. Oh I know it's supposed to be the most important day in a woman's life, but I had worked and worried so much on an empty stomach that I was in kind of a fog. Mind you, the fog lifted that night when Stanley... took his husbandly way with me. Suddenly I didn't feel like a princess anymore. So, the next morning I wrapped that dress in tissue paper and put it away in the cedar chest.

And we got on with our married life, which was surprisingly not much different from life before. I even grew to tolerate Stanley climbing on top of me at night, sometimes imagining that he was Armand Collier or Trevor St. Clair or some other movie star lover. Looking back I realise now that it never really took that long anyway, although it seemed like an eternity at the time. But it was my duty, and it would hopefully lead to something.

But it never did. After awhile, I went to old Doctor Beaton to see if I was doing something wrong. But no, he assured me that we were doing everything right. It was my body that was wrong. It could not, it would not make a baby. They used to call it barren. Like the prairie when the fields are empty. That was me. Empty, through and through.

When I got home, Stanley was still out doing the chores. To this day I don't know why, but I went to the cedar chest, took out my wedding dress and put it on. And went upstairs and sat on the bed. It was the only night in my married life when I didn't make supper.

Stanley found me sitting there. He didn't say a word. Not a peep. Stood in the doorway staring at me. I couldn't look at him, but I told him. "I can't have a baby" was all I said. Stanley was so quiet. He left the room. I stayed

. the bed, memorizing the rag rug on the floor, listening to him downstairs. A terrible racket. I thought he was breaking things, or packing to leave. I didn't know.

And then he was there again. He set something down on the bureau, walked over to me and tied an apron around me while I sat. Then he took what he had set on the bureau and put it on my lap. I looked down and there was a plate. Bacon and eggs. He knelt down, took a piece of bacon in his fingers, and held it up to my mouth. That's when we looked at each other. We stayed there for a long, long time. Me in my wedding dress and an apron, Stanley on his knees before me. Me and my man. Mr. and Mrs. Stanley Rural. Crying over a plate of bacon and eggs.

"The MisAdventures of Pussy Boy"
Alec Butler

The story of a transgendered teenager named Alick, who was born a girl yet is taken for a boy.

ALICK

When I was twelve I tantalised myself with fantasies about K.
K was sixteen, the junior high slut. She didn't take any shit.
First thing she told me was she was half French, half Indian, Métis.
Her skin was light brown like my mother's.
K was the first girl who asked me if I was half Indian.
K was the first person to ask me if I really wanted to be a boy.
We were on our way to a party to smoke dope. With boys.
Genetic boys with cool albums like Black Sabbath and Pink Floyd.
It was 1971, the dead of winter.
We trudged through a big white field surrounded by birch trees,
Bundled up in our fringed cowboy jackets and bell-bottomed hipsters.
The birch trees white ghosts gleaming in the moonlight,
Encouraging me to tell K how I felt about her.
She asked me if I wanted to be a boy. I said no.
Next thing I knew I was on my back in the snow looking up at a full moon.
K on top of me, pinning me down. Her Madonna face above me with the moon behind it like a halo. Her hot breath warmed the cold skin on my cheek, the sound of her breathing filled my ears.
The beauty mark above her French lips never looked so hot.
"You really wanna be a boy don't you," she purrs.
"No."
She starts to get off me, I pull her back, "I mean yes. Yes."
Our bodies touch full on for the first time.
The body I lusted after for months is in my arms, I don't wanna let her go.

My dream comes true and she kisses me full on the mouth, sinks her teeth
into my lower lip, bites lightly.
My crotch flash-floods all hot and wet.
"Show me what a boy you are," she hisses in my ear, daring me.
She hauls me on top of her, I rub my crotch against hers.
She starts breathing with little catches in her breath and soft cries in her
throat. I'm so in love I wanna die.
I call her "baby" she holds me tighter. I grind her harder and faster.
She wraps her arms around me tight and cries, "oh you're such a good boy."
I could feel the tension in her body, the heat of her, the need of her.
Feel the seams of our jeans rubbing together.
The harder I ride her the tighter she holds on.
I bury my face in her neck. I suck, bite, grind for all I'm worth.
Leave my mark on her.
She cries out, trembles violently all over, flops lifeless back on the snow.
Suddenly with superhuman strength she pushes me off her and rolls me
over onto my back, her face above me full of lust.
She reaches down to rub my crotch, I push her hand away.
Her hand comes back, I push it away again.
She smiles, "Come on, Pussy Boy. Doncha wanna handjob?"

After that, after I let her touch me I had trouble hiding my feelings.
Publicly she kept her distance, in class I sent her notes begging her to meet
me in the tunnels in the basement. Finally she sent me a note telling me the
coast was clear.
I made my way to the tunnels where I was taken by surprise, three on one.
The echoes of vicious words and sickening thuds swam in my head as
I made my way to the alcove where K wanted to meet.
But she wasn't there, waiting in the shadows for me.
I felt alone, betrayed by my body.
I started to howl softly with the throbbing pain, just then I heard K's
footsteps at the tunnel entrance.
My howling got louder, her footsteps picked up speed.
She ducked into the alcove and hugged me tight, finally she pulled back
and looked at me, tears spilled down her face.
She touched the bruising around my eye and very gently kissed the swollen
half of my bottom lip.

She told me to tell her what they said, I couldn't, I was too ashamed.
She insisted, "Tell me," she said, pulling on my new beard.
"Sick," I said through trembling lips, then I broke "sick.
They said I was sick."
She took me into her loving arms, stroking me with her light touch,
"Ah, yes," she said, "You and me both Baby. You and me both."
I gasped and shuddered, amazed at how she knew just what to say.
She held me tight and cooed in my ear, "Yes, you're my sick boy, you are."

"Myra"
from

Tempting Providence
Robert Chafe

Nurse Myra Grimsley leaves England in 1921 for Canada, on a contract to be the sole health care provider for three hundred square miles of sparsely settled Newfoundland coast. Here, Myra travels 60 miles with her husband and his injured brother to save his life.

MYRA

I am walking. There is no time to stop. There is no time to pause and properly survey my surroundings. I am walking and my head is turning and eyes are scanning and I see nothing. Oh God I see nothing. Countless times I have made this trip, or others like it. We have done this before. But never, never when I have travelled with Angus have I seen the emptiness. The vastness of what we are trying to conquer. Never has a distance seemed so great or impassable. Never have I felt secretly, so secretly that I will not make it. That this vastness will be the end of me. Of us. Of Alex. I am watching Angus and his bravery, and Alex and his pain, and I am feeling so thoroughly… afraid. I will admit it. Terrified of where I am. Where I have gotten myself. I love Angus, I do not doubt that, but I am having fear attack me on all sides. My God there is nothing out here, and this man, this man, my brother, Alex, his foot, his life rest with me. And I have known that responsibility, I have held that power in my hands, fought it, conquered it, lost to it. But now, here, I don't want to live if I lose. I cannot live to see Alex die, to see Angus see Alex die. I am afraid like never before, because I've never had so much to lose. I've never had so much to lose. I will not lose this, Angus! I will not lose this! Angus!

"Mother, Mother"
Florence Gibson

Nora, a young medical intern, wearing a lab coat and stethoscope, on her cell phone.

NORA

Pearson? Look, I'm in some kinda trouble down here with a little Trixie who's punched a hole in her gut with a fistful of aspirin. More than a hundred pills, then six hours sitting on a park bench till somebody notices this woman is *not* coming in out of the rain.

What's in it for you? A hole in her gastric antrum the size of my fist, that's what. No, we already did the surgery, my problem is now her pH is fucked, and I don't mean her shampoo either.

Drags on her cigarette.

Tried that.

Tried that too.

I *have* an N.G. tube, I *have* a monitor, it's her fucking pH that's the problem so–.

I called medicine: she's surgery: you're surgery. And I'm your intern okay? Okay okay look: I'm over my head okay? So just get your ass outa bed and come down here and help me out okay?

Hangs up. Butts her cigarette. Checks watch. Dials.

Chemistry? I need those repeat blood gases on—what's-her-name—ASA OD in ICU... what.

Scrambles for pen and paper.

Could you repeat those numbers?

Pause.

That's incompatible with life.

No, no, it's okay, I'm going there now.

Hangs up but doesn't move. Dials.

Pearson? Pearson are you awake because if you're not I–. What the fuck are you doing in emerg? I *told* you, this *girl,* her *gases,* you have to *come–.* Fuck—he's hung up, fuck.

Stares at phone. Slowly dials.

ICU? I'm just checking on the status of that…

(goes quiet) Yeah.

Yeah.

Okay yeah.

Quietly hangs up. Deep breath. Dials.

Hi sir hi, sorry to call you at home at a time like this but I–. Three-thirty sir I know sir but I had trouble reaching the resident, MVA in emerg, but it's this problem with the aspirin overdose sir she's–.

No sir, the surgery is fine sir it's just her pH is so off that her breathing is kind of–.

History sir? Well, somebody found her I think, park bench, expensive clothes, two small kids running around—but the police have them now. Psychiatry saw her first then sent her back to us vomiting blood and…

No sir, no, I don't think she's anybody's wife.

Well sir I didn't get involved on that level, I'm surgery, so I did the N.G. tube and she—no sir, it's not an excuse I'm just telling you I had to put the tube down, and she's young and she's strong and she fought me, to hold her down when I didn't want to, she made me, get the tube down and pump her out and make her behave like I'm supposed to and–.

No sir, no, I don't have any kids.

Yes sir.

Yes sir.

Yes sir.

Yes sir.

Hangs up, remains in stillness. Dials.

Psychiatry, I need to talk to psychiatry.

Nora Barnes, surgery. I need you to find next of kin on that aspirin overdose.

I *can't* ask her, she's comatose.

Calgary, a mother in Calgary, that's all I got.

How should *I* know who you're going to talk to? That's not my job, I mean, she comes in here, eleventh hour, all blood and fucked and a *coma* and it's time to *talk*? I mean we controlled the bleeding as far as I'm concerned— and this is why I went into surgery in the first place, so *you* guys could do the talking. She's crazy, neurotic, and I'm supposed to *fix* that, fix her like you fix the damn *cat*? I'm fighting her, I'm holding her down and all she can say is, "I fucked up so bad, with my kids, with my life." And I'm supposed to *talk* about this? Talk while I'm ramming a tube down her throat? And then, from the chief: "Have I got kids?" Well no, sir, no, sorry but I don't, my mother had enough of them for *both* of us. You think I don't know how far from that park bench I'd be if I was running around crazy after kids? She's nuts, she's psych, she grabs me by the stethoscope and says, "You wear this instead of a necklace?"

Because I had to say to her, "Sorry about the pearls." They went all over the floor when the string broke. The nurse in emerg said they were genuine.

She's got me two inches from her face and she says, "Why don't you just let go?" But she won't take the tube, and I have to sit on her chest, and the nurse ties her down. "I bet your mother's proud of you," she says, "I bet she turned out just like me, and you're gonna turn out like her."

Not in a million years. Not my mother, no sir, with her lace curtains and her thick, thick blinds, she had herself convinced that her friends on the ladies' auxiliary were planting bombs in the baba-o-rhum cakes. And she'd finger her pearls, she'd run her fingers up and down them like elevators. Always wanting to talk, as soon as Dad would leave to go on his rounds, she'd scream the house down with her talk, talk, talk, she keeps talking to me—she talks to me from the *grave*—I want her to stop talking to *me*.

Silence.

You can't be there for everybody.

If you're going to live up to being a doctor you can't be there for everybody.

Silence.

(softly) She has to have a tube down her throat.

I can't just let go.

So I don't know why she would say that. I don't know why she would say that to me.

> *NORA stares at the phone. Hangs up. She runs her fingers up and down her stethoscope.*

"Katherine"
from

Ospedaletti
Janice Kulyk Keefer

These monologues are part of a play focusing on the short story writer Katherine Mansfield and her companion Ida Baker, who spent a tortuous winter in Ospedaletti, on the Italian Riviera, in 1918-19. Mansfield, terminally ill with pulmonary tuberculosis, hoping to survive the winter in a warmer climate than London offered, is coming to terms with the destruction of all her hopes for personal happiness, and is summoning the will and acquiring the integrity to write the work that will touch the truth of life, as she has glimpsed it, as harsh and harrowing as that truth may be.

KATHERINE

I

 (*mimicking the dopey voice, half cheerful, half mournful of Ida Baker, her nurse and companion*) "No mail again, Katie!" You're happy that he hasn't written aren't you, you're like a cow in clover, or a vulture at the feeding trough. Ida Baker the undertaker—the born Layer Out, the Albatross: that's you. A thousand things to do in this hellhole villa, fires to light, tea to boil up, carrots to scrape, lamps to trim and all you can do is sit there watching me, waiting for me to cough, waiting for my fever to spike, for my joints to ache so that I can't even crawl from my bed to the bath. Because the more helpless I am, the more I need you, and the more I need you the more power you have, yes you, Ida. Power over me, power to crush me to your talcum powder bosom and bloody smother me. You're not an undertaker—you're a murderer!

 K buries her head in her arms; she seems to be coughing but when she lifts her head, she is laughing.

I could never murder you; I couldn't even shoot you. "I could never make your body into a neat parcel and put it under the stones" or wrap you up in your greasy apron and throw you into the fire—oh no Ida, not you, you'd never burn—you're the kind that will live for a hundred and fifty years!

What's worse, what's a thousand times worse is how you feed on me—you're swollen sick with me, you've swallowed me whole because you haven't any self of your own. You haven't a thought in your head, a single desire you haven't filched from me! Do you think I don't see you with your eyes fixed on me—fixed—waiting for what I shall do next, say next, so that you can store it up and copy it? I cannot stand the look of you, the weight of you, the appetite! Stop eating me—stop pulling up to this sick, starved table and gorging on me!

No, Ida, this isn't my sickness speaking, it isn't blood I'm spitting up at you now but the truth. I don't want to be patient with you, I don't want to remember the old days together, I don't want to give it a week, a month, a year so that we can go back to what we were—I haven't got a week or month or year. By God, I shall cut my throat if I haven't cut yours tonight! I warn you, I will get away with murder. Because it's myself that I'll be killing, not you but your blubbery reflection of who I am, who I could have been. If you could see yourself now—if you could see your "great fat arms, [your] tiny blind breasts, [your] baby mouth and that underlip"—God—"always wet and a crumb or two of chocolate stain at the corners."

> *K drags herself over to a large mirror on the sitting-room wall; she walks with the aid of a stick, like an old, old woman. She stares into the mirror and addresses the face she finds there.*

"The worst thing about hate is that it never spends itself—is never exhausted, and in this case isn't even shared. So you come up against something which says hit me, hate me, hate me, feel strongly about me… it doesn't matter which way as long as I make you feel." And it's all I can feel, all this rotting, crippled body allows me to feel—"Christ, to hate like I do."

II

(speaking to her younger self) So, the wild colonial girl has ended up taking the veil. Look at you—lying in that ridiculous bed, swathed in mosquito netting like some mummified martyred priestess. At the ripe old age of thirty-one, queen of the living dead. Lie awake all night, rise at noon; struggle down to lunch—lie on the sofa till six, then ask the Albatross for your hot water bottle—and drag yourself back up to bed. Mrs. Jack Murry, nobody's wife, mother of none. Author of some satiric sketches that you've now disowned, and a failed novel masquerading as a long short story. Author of your own untimely end. As Mother would say, you've brought it all on yourself: headstrong, disobedient, careless girl!

Think of it, think of yourself, only ten years ago: a stunt girl in an American movie, a nightclub performer, a Moody-Manners chorus girl. Careless, all right—so careless you got yourself pregnant and then managed to lose the baby. And picked up a nasty disease along the way, as well as a husband or two; one you left on your wedding night, the other turns his face away when you come up to kiss him. You were full of beans and full of bacilli, you used to say—well, the beans are long gone and the bacilli? They've eaten you up so there's hardly a scrap left of you for Ida to take care of. Ida, your wife, your albatross, your only faithful friend—Ida ought to murder you in your bed, the way you treat her. She ought to take this little gun and aim straight at whatever heart you've got left—shoot right through those rotting holes in your lungs. It's not fever you're burning up with Katherine, it's hate.

You're not strong enough to hold a pen; your husband turns away from you from fear of catching what's killing you. Every breath you take you owe to the goodness of someone you can't stand the sound or sight of. What a plunge, what a crash! Eighteen, and you were striking out for power, freedom, glory; thirty now, and all you can think of is how you will scrape one more breath from your bones.

And you lie here alone, and you think of everything you've lost and everything you've left undone. The wind screams, the waves grind against the shore, and you are smaller than a pebble; the waves suck you in and under and no one will save you, no one will come in to comfort you, and it will never, never be morning.

"January"
from

Last Stop for Miles
Celia McBride

January comes to tell Thomson the story of the murder of his ex-girlfriend, Cherokee. After she avoids telling him the truth by seducing him and then running off, she returns to finally confess what happened.

JANUARY

We got to Slow Pete's cabin and the guys started taking their clothes off and more booze and… I couldn't even see straight. I'd been sick in the truck. And all of a sudden I hear Kee say, "Don't." And I look over and Pete is roping her to this chair and her shirt is open and he's squeezing her breasts and… I woke up. All of a sudden I'm sober and I get up and run over to help her or do something, untie her or something and Slow Pete tells Paul to hold me back. He goes, "Hold that little girl's cuntie awhile." And Paul yanks my arms behind my back and as soon as Kee sees Paul's got me she wakes up, too. "What the fuck are you doing! Let go of my friend!" And Pete whacks her with this zipper thing it… had sections like a snake it… was very heavy steel and… I thought it broke her neck and I hear Dean or someone say, "Hey Pete, what the fuck?" And Pete grins this psycho grin and tells us he's going to set things straight with his wife, right? I mean his wife! "She's not your wife, Pete! For fuck sake!" And he takes out his knife, this great big knife with a huge black handle and he sticks it into Kee's stomach. Just like that. No warning, no anything. He sticks it right here, high up under her ribs. And we heard it. Going in it made this sound. This terrible sound. A quiet ripping sound. *(pause)* The whole room was completely still. And Kee… she's looking at me and… we're in each other's dream. Everything disappeared. *(pause)* And then Pete grabs the handle and he pulls it out, yanks it out and the blade and she screamed and everything moved again. Fast. I ran toward Kee and Pete swung me around and pushed me down hard and yelled at the guys to get out and he shoved his big dirty hand down my pants. And I… I peed. I peed on his hand and he smiled and his disgusting tongue came at me and I saw this big white bump way at the back like an overgrown tastebud and… I retched. But then all of a sudden he's off me and I look up and there's Dean standing above me all his skin very white. He's holding the zipper thing. It's swinging above me and Pete is out cold and… something… an animal. Her. In me. I jumped on top of him screaming and raging my hands squeezing his throat. Dean didn't stop me. None of them did. *(pause)* The room started spinning in circles and I could see a deer head going around and other things and Kee… it wasn't her. She'd left the body, you know? Then I passed out. *(pause)* When I awoke, the guys had thrown him in the river. Murder-suicide right? Cops bought it. Well. They knew but…

"Paco and the Shoes"
Monique Mojica

A woman enters, furtive. She is in her fifties—an *abuelita*. She could have a stall selling herbs and candles in the market or she could be the one people come to to cure headaches, heartaches, diarrhea. The one who is awakened at all hours when there are babies to be caught, so she knows the names of all the children in the neighbourhood. She wears a *rebozo* and hugs to her chest a market bag with handles. She freezes, listening. When she is certain no sound can betray her whereabouts, she upturns the market bag and shoes of all colours and sizes come tumbling out. Her hands compelled by memory and by what her grandmother has taught her, she spreads her *rebozo* on the ground and places the shoes side by side on top of it. Also in her bag is a rope and a small smudge pot which she lights. She smudges herself, caressing her body with the smoke as if washing. She prays.

He said, (he said, he said, he said, he said)
        "The first time I saw a dead body–
            I was six years old."

        Memory as gaping wound.
What sutures will bring the jagged edges
        of torn flesh   together?
Will it scab over? Only to leave a fiery,
        raised and angry scar?
        Or–
    will the skin never renew itself–
        but remain a thin blue membrane
            fragile
        and prone to bursting open
            to reveal
        the boiling blood just beneath the surface–

unable to contain
the memory
a moment longer?

He told me, (he said, he said, he said, he said)
"I always knew when there'd been a
massacre
by the shoes..."

I see the scattering of forlorn shoes
abandoned in the plaza

> *One by one she passes each shoe through the smoke to purify and*
> *bless it. She smudges the rope also, then begins to tie each shoe onto*
> *the rope as an offering and prayer.*

orphaned
left to lie on their sides/upside-down
empty of feet that gave them life
and movement

A man's oxford here, a sneaker there
but mostly women's shoes
tacones
pink, turquoise, white and black high heels
debris
left behind to litter the square
the only evidence of
the hungry, vicious teeth of
automatic weapon fire.
A boot here, a *caite* there.

Did they jump straight up out of those shoes?
I wonder.
Did they have time to bend to untie them?
Did they struggle to squirm a foot out
over the back of the shoe with a
desperate heel?

Did they step on glass as they ran?
as they fell

> as they heard
> breath expelled around them?

Did they run blindly on unprotected feet
> along asphalt and cobblestone?
Did they know their lonely shoes had relations
> in the pile of detritus
> from the Death Camps
> now catalogued, acquisitioned, and museumed?

Or, did they simply lie there
> choking on their own entrails
> while their shoes–
> > mouths yawning death masks/ their shoes
> called out to
> their lost owners and
schoolchildren counted the dead from
> beneath half-closed eyelids
> as their books were searched
> on their way home from school?

He said, (he said, he said, he said, he said)
> "I always knew when there'd been a
> > massacre
> by the shoes…"

She picks up the rope with the shoes tied to it, wraps it around her body, and drags it off behind her. She takes them to a safe place where they will not be desecrated.

"I am Sad, Still"
Monique Mojica

A woman sleeps. She could be in her own bed, she could be on the subway; she could have lain her head down on her desk for a moment. She dreams. She sees. She keeps trying to sleep. She wakes with a start over and over.

A jolt like electricity–

I wake up–
>   suffocating my mouth and nose filled with dirt.
>   Was I dreaming again of drowning?
>   of being crushed against the ceiling of
>   a room suddenly shrinking?
>   It's hard to breathe so I breathe as little as possible.
>   My legs are cramped and I have to pee.

I wake up–
>   I am in Canada   chunks of earth in my nostrils
>   roots poking into my side
>   I taste dirt   and something else…

I wake up–
>   I see the man's face—impassive   calm
>   He looks into the camera
>   releases a breath

I wake up–
>   I am in Canada   gasping to breathe against
>   the dust   and smell of blood
>   "*Bueno*," he tells the cameraman,
>   "I will show you where I hid."

An *arroyo*   flies still buzzing around the stick drying blood
       buzzing   thick
where the bullets swarmed thick around the people of the bees
      Las Abejas.
The camera moves to…   women's shoes   two pairs
      carefully set side by side.
There is a small cave in the bank of the *arroyo*
      crumbling earth   dark
    "*Aqui, señores*," he says,"here I hid as if I were dead
        saved
      two   of my children.
     I am sad still
     My wife was killed with another child. My sister, two
     brothers in law, three nephews."
I wake up–
    I am in Canada   we lie very still   chunks of earth in our
      nostrils   and mouths
        not breathing—not moving
        I have to pee.
        Ten hours
   In this hole   three of us lie.
   Outside   screams
     outside   hack hack CHUN   of the machetes
    bullets buzzing   swarms of bullets
        swarms of flies

  Bullets made in Canada
  M16s assembled in Canada
        bullets swarm like flies

  Pace quickens, fighting hysteria
I wake up–
    I am suffocating   my mouth and nose filled with dirt.
    My legs are cramped and I have to pee.
I wake up–
    I am in Canada
I wake up–
    on a pile of dead

Gesture—flung backwards spread eagle.

I wake up–

in the snow at Wounded Knee/

Gesture—frozen twisted like Bigfoot.

hiding along the riverbank at Batoche/

Gesture—crouched down covering head.

being crushed in a boxcar to Treblinka

Gesture—arms in front palms forward pressing.

Three gestures repeated alone:

Flung backwards spread eagle.
Frozen twisted like Bigfoot.
Crouched down covering head.
Arms in front palms forward pressing.

I wake up–

I am in Acteal
December 22, 1997
and I am sad still.

from

Cut Me

M. Nourbese Phillip

A room with a hospital bed, an intravenous unit and a bathtub filled with fragrant leaves. A woman sings.

WOMAN

> *Ah north, ah south, ah east, ah west*
> *I took my boyfriend to the candy store*
> *He bought me ice cream, he bought me cake*
> *He brought me home with a belly ache*
> *Mama, Mama, I'm so sick*
> *Call the doctor quick quick quick*
> *Doctor, doctor, will I die*
> *Close your eyes and count to five*
> *ah one ah two ah three ah four ah five*
> *I'm alive.*

It's bad enough, you lose control. Your body's not doing what you want it to do. Or doing what you don't want it to do. It's betraying you. But then you have to give it up. To someone else. To do something with. Even something small. Like having a lump removed. From your breast. They've assured you it'll be all right. They're pretty sure it's benign. But still, there you are, before cock crow as they say back home, in this huge concrete building with lots of strange people. White people for the most part. And this man—this white man in a white coat. He is going to cut my breast. Open. To help me. I have to—I suspend all my atavistic fears about him being white. And male. He is kind. Calls me by my first name. Pats me. He likes me. I want him to like me! I am suddenly in a strangely intimate relationship with him. This white man. He is going to cut me. And I am going to let him. Cut me. Wide open. Does he understand the leap of faith? Is it? Or merely the leap of "I got no choices but this one?" I won't let them put me under, though. I want to know what's happening. At all times. If you're going to cut me—if I am going to let you cut me, I should at least know, shouldn't I? They sedate me. Give me a local. Oh but I can still feel pain. A lot of pain.

He reaches right inside my breast. I can feel him mucking around in there. Pulling and tugging. I hear him say to the doctor in training, "I want to get it all." I want to get it all.

He wants to get it all!

He can't get it all.

Ever.

He can't ever–

from

Rabid

Kevin Rees

Kelly, a nineteen-year-old member of a gang of neo-Nazi skins is at the police station. She is being interrogated about the death of her lover Eddy, the leader of the gang.

KELLY

I'm sick. Not that kind of sick. I know what I hate. You ever hate something so much it makes you sick? One day you just feel different, then maybe indifferent, and then time passes and you realise that there is something really rotten in you, just hanging out, being what it is, a small something of a nothing. A bitty little black burning ball in the pit of your heart, or groin, or gut. Call it a seed, I dunno, a sprout, a spore—whatever you want. This thing is gestating, multiplying itself, splitting itself in two, in two, in two and two and on and on—then it becomes more complex, not just bigger but more complicated—ALIVE! You remind yourself why it's there and you cry and punch shit cause you just have no goddamn… idea! You wonder what it will look like if it comes out. Then it starts to talk. It talks to you, at first, sweetly. "Hi Honey, How are you? Good, that's good, listen, you're right and they are wrong." THEN LIKE YOU'RE AN IDIOT!, it'll insult you as it writhes its way up from your gut and through your liver… SWIMMING IN BOOZE AND IT'S DRUNK AND IT CHOKES ON THE SMOKE IN YOUR LUNGS… your lungs. You breathe it out and in, it's your rhythm, slightly, softly it sounds its name in your ear. Quietly. Just enough to make you shiver… and doubt it. Then it starts to pay you visits when you don't know it's comin', starts to tell you shit—in History class, in the hall, at the store. It's in the head now, hanging around in the back somewhere belching words at you, in you, about you, about the new neighbours, the cab driver, the funny smelling store at the strip mall—the part-timers who forced your dad into early retirement. I know this, I know where it comes from, it's contagious. I know who, what, where, when, but I don't know how. I don't know.

from

The Knife-Thrower's Partner
Douglas Burnet Smith

The woman speaking is the partner of the knife-thrower in a third-rate, travelling carnival or circus. She speaks of what it's like to stand there, night after night, and have someone throw knives lethally close to her body.

THE PARTNER

He gets to wear the blindfold, I get to see the flashing blades and bone handles flying at me. I never hear them swish past my temples, or thud just under my sequined crotch; I hear only mosquitoes out for blood after a rain. I try to ignore the nervous laughter of the audience, those owls refusing to blink, and when I walk away from the plywood backstop it is not my outline there in knives, it is the outline of a woman who stiffens at the sound of cutlery, a woman who has worn the same costume for years, unaware that underneath there is a body trembling. Before each performance I tear a page out of the Bible, burn it, rub the ashes into my hair.

Imagine you're a diamond and someone starts picking at the wall all around you, no light on his helmet, and you harden until you shatter like a window. It burns. I nearly black out, and when I come to, the ball of yellow light barrels across the stage, covers me with pollen. Ever wake up, and first thing, almost without noticing, draw your nails across your belly and hear a razor blade opening a wrist, and know that sound is just an echo and that your whole life is just a bunch of goddamn echoes and someone else is doing all the talking?

I had raw knuckles. They ached for anything, danger danger. I wanted a Clyde. I'd be Bonnie. He was smoothtalk-fasthands-daredevil so I went off with him, left the dust to diesel itself in that one-room dump—someone else's dirt in the tub from someone else's neck. Got a house-on-wheels, saw the country. Every now and then he gave me a little money to gamble with. Hooch whenever I wanted, from Rubber Man. But not him. Never. "I told ya, I can't touch that stuff!" He'd yell me back along that narrow hallway to the bedroom. The walls papered with crescent moons, scimitars I'd drift off watching, after he'd drained himself into the darkness.

I can walk out there and sometimes those knives are just sparrows bickering at my ears, as if *their* hearts were the only ones beating. I'm like some moth, frozen by the lights, but between the fear, and the fear *of* the fear, there's this clearing of white flowers where an unbelievable life makes sense, and I know I'm composed of millions of pieces, and when I stand this still those pieces knit, close over and my blood moves sure.

Being a boy would have been so much easier. Just take your shirt off if you're hot. Just pee right there if you have to pee. Say whatever you like to the teacher, be a hero when she straps you six times on each hand hard at the front of the room for throwing snowballs at the girls. The only good thing about being a girl was that when you grew up, you got to strap boys.

from

Perfect Pie
Judith Thompson

Francesca (Marie) has asked Patsy what it is like to have an epileptic seizure.

PATSY

What are they like what are they like I would like to say they're like going to sleep in fact that is what I tell people, don't want to worry them, but Marie I live in fear. I live in fear of the next seizure it's like there's a stalker. And he's always there, parked in the driveway, in his old car, waiting. I come down to turn out the lights his face, in the window, his eyes, goin through me, I am out in the fields on the tractor, there he is, behind the tree, with his knife and his dirty long fingernails all for me, waiting, and sometimes, if I've had too much wine, or not enough sleep, he will walk towards me. Last week, in the Kingston Shopping Centre, there he was comin out of the Cotton Ginny Plus store, smiling, smoking and he comes towards me and the floor starts moving and I'm lookin around I'm saying oh my God no, no, somebody help me my God and the walls are shifting and my stomach is turning I'm about to throw up and he keeps walking towards me, he is going to kill me…. Now, everybody, people are staring, I put my head between my knees, "Are you alright, lady? Can I get you a glass of water?" And they don't seem to see him he is right on top of me, his scrawny arms around me his breath like vomit in my face his eyes burning me and he holds me so close like constricting, and crushing and I'm trying to yell but they can't hear my voice because he's over my face and he is pulling and pulling me closer… can't breathe…. Can't breathe now and the people are so far away it's like he is moving me under the floor, the linoleum-marble floor and under the mall and the people and into the dark the pipes and the loneliness and they are all so far away and

I will die under this floor like a cockroach all my life over, all over and he will be filled up with me and then, then, suddenly, the way someone who's been underwater just kinda pops out and the water falls off them I am there, on the floor of the mall, and the air, and the people around me, and the ambulance guys, and I sit up, I tell em it's okay, just a seizure, but I got these needles in my head, and I drink a Sprite someone's got for me, and I tell the nice lady who's a nurse that I'm okay, and the staring children, and I get myself up, and I'm shakin', yes, and wobbly, but I gotta do my shopping, gotta get it down, only come to Kingston once a month and I walk down the mall, and into the Grand & Toy, got to get supplies for the books, and he is there. There he is, behind the paper, just staring, oh he wants me back. Could be another seizure, see, that's the thing, the more you have them, the more you have them, your brain remembers that's what my doctor said, so he knows, Stalker knows he could get me again. He stands there, Marie, he stands there lickin his dry lips, waiting, waiting with his dirty fingers to hold me too close and move me under and he knows; he knows that he can get me any time he wants.

from

Capture Me
Judith Thompson

DELPHINE

Yes. I thought you might ask about that… it's so long ago now
I… well it's not something I like to think about, Jerry, because it was… it
was really not… it was one of those… I grew up in a very strict Catholic
family, you understand, on the east coast in a very small town I was very
sheltered I didn't know what an erection was until I was sixteen; truly,
imagine me, Delphine Moth, fourteen years old, I hadn't ever HAD
a period, I was a really late bloomer, I had about two days of pains, so
I thought I was finally going to menstruate like my friends, but then I was
in Geography class giving a little talk on volcanoes, I remember exactly
what I was saying, I was saying, on "the Island of Krakatoa, the volcano
erupted in 1867 killing 36,000 souls." And suddenly I felt this terrific pain
and I said, "Excuse me I am not feeling well at all if you don't mind may
I be excused Sister Barney?" That was her name. And so I ran down the
hallway to the washroom and I went into the stall and then the pain well
I'm sure you've heard what labour is like. I felt I became a Krakatoa I felt
like I was a mountain in a very cold a freezing country a tall pink and red
mountain and I thought I heard drums and the drums were drumming
louder and louder and the people the women were singing the air was
darkening the pressure in my head the pain the pure horror of pain.
I couldn't scream, the janitor Bill would hear me. I bit on my arm and it
was as if the volcano exploded and the people ran ran in their bare feet the
hot hot lava catching them, drowning them, she was drowning in the lava
she had to get away get away from the lava, she she pulled herself away,
looked into the white round pool and there was a bloody creamy the lava
had killed a child she bit she bit off the vine that had strangled the child
she picked up the child she would save the child she she heard a mewling
a crying run run away they are coming after the baby they want to sacrifice

the baby running down the hall "Miss Moth, Miss Moth may I ask where you might be?" Catch the bus the bus goes way out only two of us on the bus blood running down my legs feeling dizzy very dizzy okay, Come and Stay A While campground run down the long long driveway, past the few trailers to the fairground, my blood running down my legs all over the ground saw the Ferris wheel the rusting Ferris wheel and I saved the baby I put her on the Ferris wheel away from harm from the hot hot lava and "Krakatoa Girl" ran all the way back to the school on the hot lava sliding sliding for a typing test. Mother said I had to do well in typing if I wanted to be a doctor. Mr. Hale the typing teacher with the goatee and the white shoes, he noticed that blood was dripping onto the floor below me. "Oh no, that's just lava said I, I was just in a volcano explosion you know, over the island on the island." All the kids were talking behind their hands, and Sister Johnny she put her hands on my shoulders and I blacked right out and I didn't come to light until I was in hospital. In mental hospital there was a horse in my room and a small volcano.

> *Beat.*

My older cousin Shelley she sat there with me for weeks; she held my hand, she helped me breathe and said "Never never feel guilty; you did nothing wrong." I did nothing wrong. I did nothing wrong. I am not responsible for you.

I'm sorry.

"The Morning Bird"
Colleen Wagner

Doreen, a street person, has stolen a jacket from the hospital and waits outside hoping to discover the owner without having to give up the jacket.

DOREEN sits on a step outside a hospital admitting area with an unlit cigarette in her mouth. She wears an expensive designer jacket which she pulls around her to keep out the cold, and digs her hands deep into the pockets. She discovers something and pulls it out— a lighter, a silver one with a flip lid. She is impressed and sets it down on the step beside her and looks at it. She picks it up with precision and moves it closer to her. She takes the cigarette out of her mouth and uses it to point at the lighter.

DOREEN

(*imitating Robert DeNiro in "Taxi Driver"*) "You talking to me? I said, are you talking to me?"

The winter is no time to get sick I'm telling you. Freeze your butt off waiting for doctors. And what do they tell you—"you're pretty sick. Come back next week if you're not feeling any better."

Sure eh. How long you gonna do that before you get the message?

They always take X-rays when you're sick. Those doctors can't tell nothing without exposing your bones to radiation. "It's safe," they say. "Less radiation than you get when you're in an airplane." I don't fly. Ever. For just that reason. Look what it's done to all those people in Chernobyl!

We were told not to eat any cheese coming out of that part of the world, but I bet lots of people are. Radiation loves cheese. Anything with fat. And it stays there forever. And there are those people eating all that cheese thinking it's real good for them but what they don't tell them is it's full of radiation which causes cancer and babies to be born with two heads–

Pulls the jacket around her.

I love the spring. All the birds coming back. I love the robins. I heard China doesn't have any birds left except the ones in cages. That's because the farmers complained that the birds were eating all their grain so Chairman Mao told everyone to get out there and kill them. And they did. And that's a lot of people—billions—going after a few birds.

And birds don't migrate there anymore. *(laughs)* I guess they got the message.

(remembering) Oh yeah! X-rays! So they X-ray me. They take me down to the bottom of the hospital in this cold dark room that smells funny. Know that smell? The smell of metal and tungsten light and they put me on a metal table and twist my legs around and they shone this square light on me with a black cross through it like a window with four panes, and it's framing my abdomen and they push a button even though I'm telling them I'm not ready—and they push it anyway because nobody in the basement hears me because all the metal down there has made them deaf, so they push the button even though I'm screaming now "I'M NOT READY!" and the table vibrates and the radiation shoots through me like invisible bullets and all the tiny molecules and atoms are blown to smithereens because radiation does that but most of the time we don't feel it unless we're sensitive and the doctors don't even think about it because all they want is a good clear shot of your bones but they got to get through everything else to get there. Like your heart even to get through to your spine!

I died then and there on that table. I died and woke up in a hospital bed someone else.

she

speaks

CHILDHOOD MEMORIES

"Rebecca"
from

The Unnatural and Accidental Women
Marie Clements

Rebecca reflects on the death of her father, and how they were affected by her mother's departure.

REBECCA

My dad—The Character was still full-limbed but hard-of-hearing when he died. Still asking "Eh?" after every sentence I spoke, but quick to hear the sound of change falling to the ground. Death was no big surprise for him. The thing he couldn't get out from under was the day she left. I found him holding a piece of paper she had put on the kitchen table. He held it for a long time and then simply folded it and put it in his pocket. "Where's Mom?" I asked.

SFX: sound of tree falling and landing.

He said, "She went for a walk." I thought maybe she had gone to the IGA or something. Somebody was always having to go to the IGA. When she didn't return and he didn't move, I started complaining about the big fact that I was supposed to get new running shoes today. I was supposed to go downtown today. I was supposed to get a hamburger today… milkshakes, fries and ketchup at Woolworth's. It was supposed to have been a great day, and now we had to wait. I was getting pissed off, because I was getting tired of going to The Salvation Army for smelly clothes, and I felt like I was gonna be normal like everyone else when Mom said we could go to The Army and Navy and get something new, something that smelled good, something that nobody had every worn. Blue suede running shoes—three stripes on either side. I had to have them. It was unbearable, and my dad just standing there, and my mom deciding to go to IGA. I thought it was a master plan. Both of them against me being normal. I started yelling— the injustice was too great. My dad just stood there like he didn't hear anything. "Get in the truck," he said. We went. I ate hamburgers and floats and fries and everything I could see in the posters of food on the walls of the Woolworth's cafeteria on Hastings Street. We went to The Army and Navy. We went home. No Mom. Again.

"Where's Mom?" again. He said, "She left us, I didn't know anything was wrong." He sat down. I took my running shoes off. I would never wear them again. Nothing was going to be normal.

"Then Down There"
from

Songs of Want
Randi Helmers

— ⊚ — ⊚ —

mom brother dog me
White House Inaugural Ball tv American Tune
"Goodnight" brother dog mom me "See you in the morning"
time to get up "Time to get up—*Henry Al-drich*—you're going to be late"
OH GOD   HELP ME   HELP   GOD   ME
what *(bark like a dog)*
dad down there   find brother
HOLD HIM UP! CUT HIM DOWN!
what   what   hanging?
mom s w i n g   s w i n g   s w i n g   two-by-four
oh god *(bark)*
me run up   grab phone "help" breathe "your name?"
"help—dead—HE'S DEAD HE'S DEAD HE'S" "what?" "HANGED HE'S"
(bark) "what is your name?" "TRY TO REVIVE HIM!"
Carry him   Place him   mouth to rock cold mouth
thick black electrical cord   neck
knees   toilet   God   O Brother   Please bring back
dad, hold me
mom   mom   mom   silent
ambulance steals in   doctor here
"Lord giveth"   valium   "Lord taketh,"
music book open on piano   knot book open in rec room
down there   down there   down there   there there
alone   touch him   purple lines on neck   lips   *to kiss so tender*—
dead   down there   dead of night   down there
below my bed

dead
down there
why didn't I hear
down there
why didn't I know
down there
why didn't I feel
down there
why am I alive o down down
why didn't the dog bark
then
down there

In memory of Henrik O. Helmers II, Jan. 21, 1962—Jan. 20, 1977

"Indian Princess Doll"
Trisha Lamie

Once upon a time long long ago and far far away, there was
a little girl who loved dolls and that little
girl was me me me… ME

This little girl me, little me, had a mother and a father and
two sisters and an uncle

One day my uncle met a beautiful girl (woman) from
far away far far away named MeMe.

They decided to get married and go on a honeymoon…
moon… moon… moon

There is a moon in the sky
It's called the moon.

White light
Shining bright
Blood light

My uncle and my aunt MeMe went to Disneyland for their honeymoon.
When they were there they
met Mickey Mouse and Snow White and the Seven Dwarfs and
Sleeping Beauty and the Wicked Witch.
It was a magical time.

When the honeymoon was over they came home… home… home.

There's no place like home… very late one night.

There's a surprise for you little me

My aunt and uncle came home.

They brought me a surprise very late one night while I was sleeping
an
Indian
princess
doll.

They placed her in my arms while I was sleeping very late one night.

Blood light
Shining bright

When I awoke the next morning I couldn't believe my eyes...
shining bright. I thought I was dreaming.

There in my arms was an Indian princess doll.

She had long
straight
shiny
sleek
smooth
soft
black hair

She had beautiful brown eyes
She had beautiful brown skin

She was wearing a beautiful brown suede beaded and fringed
dress and a pair of beautiful brown beaded moccasins.

Breathe, Breathe, Breathe,
I can't
Sh Sh Sh Sh

I loved her
I loved my aunt.

Once upon a time, long long ago and far far away
but not as long ago or as far away as when my
aunt and uncle got married and went to
Disneyland for the honeymoon.

My aunt had a baby…girl
very late one night
while I was sleeping

When I awoke the next morning I couldn't believe my eyes
shining bright
I thought I was dreaming

There in my aunt's arms was a beautiful baby… girl

She had
straight
shiny
sleek
smooth
soft
black hair

She had beautiful brown eyes

She had beautiful brown skin

Breathe… Breathe… Breathe
I can't
Sh… Sh… Sh…
I loved her
I loved my aunt
I loved my aunt's baby

He should never have married someone from far far away, my mom said

Sh…Sh…Sh…

He should have married someone from here, my father said.

Don't tell
Don't tell
Don't tell

He should never have married, my sisters said.

But what beautiful brown eyes she has, I said
What beautiful brown hair she has, I said
What beautiful brown skin she has, I said

Just like my Indian princess doll.
Not like me
Pale face
Moon face
There's a moon in the sky…

Sh… said my mother
Sh… said my father
Sh… said my sisters

I loved my aunt
I loved my aunt's baby.

I wanted to let my aunt know.
I wanted to tell her how beautiful her baby was.

The next morning when I woke I couldn't believe my eyes

My Indian princess doll
My Indian princess doll
Where was my Indian princess doll

You're too old for dolls, said my mother
We'll buy you another doll, said my father
They threw your doll away, said my sisters

Far, far away

My eyes
Shining bright
Scary light

Don't cry… Don't cry… Don't cry

Breathe… Breathe… Breathe

Through the forest and far away
I ran
To my aunt's house

Sh… Sh… Sh…

Very softly
I crept into my aunt's house
While they were sleeping

Their beautiful baby... girl
I held her in my arms
While she was sleeping

Sh... Sh... Sh

Very softly I crept
Out of my aunt's house
While they were sleeping

Through the forest and far away
I ran
from my aunt's house
with my aunt's beautiful baby girl
to Disneyland

Don't cry... Don't cry... Don't cry

We'll live with Snow White and the Seven Dwarfs
We'll be safe and warm
We'll live happily ever after
The Wicked Witch will never find us

So cold... so dark... so... night

Sleep... Sleep... Sleep
Like Sleeping Beauty

When I awoke the next morning I couldn't believe my eyes

Where was my aunt's beautiful baby girl
Where was my beautiful Indian princess

You are a wicked, wicked child, cried my mother
You could have killed the baby, cried my father
You're banished from my house, cried my aunt

Go away and never come back

Once upon a time, there was a girl who loved dolls and
that little girl was me
But that was long long ago and far far away

from

Marion Bridge
Daniel MacIvor

Agnes sits alone on stage drinking. A flask in her bag; a suitcase beside her. She addresses the audience.

AGNES

In the dream I'm drowning. But I don't know it at first. At first I hear water and I imagine it's going to be a lovely dream. Even though every time I dream the dream I'm drowning each and every time I dream the dream I forget. Fooled by the sound of the water I guess and I imagine it's a dream of a wonderful night on the beach, or a cruise in the moonlight, or an August afternoon in a secret cove—but a moment after having been fooled into expecting bonfires or handsome captains or treasures in the weedy shore it becomes very clear that the water I'm hearing is the water that's rushing around my ears and fighting its way into my mouth and pulling me down into its dark, soggy oblivion. No captains, no treasures, no bonfires for me, no in my dream I'm drowning. And then, just when it seems it's over—that I drown and that's the dream—in the distance, on the beach, I see a child. A tall thin child, maybe nine or ten. And his sister, younger, five. Then behind them comes their mother spreading out a blanket on the sand. It's a picnic. And beside the mother is the man. Tall. Strong. And broad shoulders, good for sitting on if you're five, or even ten. Good for leaning on if you're tired, good for crying on if you're sad. And he's got his hands on his hips and he's looking out at the water, and he sees something. Me. And he reaches out and touches his wife's elbow who at that very moment sees something too and then the children, as if they're still connected to their mother's eyes, think they might see the same thing. And with all my strength—if you can call strength that strange, desperate, exhausted panic—I wave. My right arm. High. So they'll be sure to see. And they do. They see me. And then all of them, standing in a perfect line, they all wave back. The little girl, her brother, their mother and the man. They smile and wave. Then the mother returns to her blanket and the basket of food she has there, the man sits, stretching out his legs, propping himself up on one arm, the little boy runs off in search of starfish or crab shells, and the little girl smiles and waves, smiles and waves and smiles and waves. And then I drown. And that's so disturbing, because you know what they say when you die in your dream. Strange. But stranger I guess is that I'm still here.

"1979"
Celia McBride

This monologue came out of an exercise during a Master Class with Judith Thompson at Playwrights' Workshop Montreal in April 2000.

JANIE

We'd just moved to the big city. I was an incredibly innocent seven-year-old. My new school had a jogging program at lunch hour and we'd jog from the school down to the nearby ravine. It was a hot day and my friend and I were lagging behind. We got separated from the supervisor and the rest of the group. We jogged past a man staring at us from the side of the dirt road. He had his penis out and he was rubbing it. We ran on, disbelieving what we'd seen. We squealed with disgusted laughter turning back for one more look. He was running toward us. I noticed his curly black hair bobbing up and down. That moment, when you realise you're being chased… it's pure terror. We took off. But I couldn't run fast enough. Or I stopped running. To this day I can't be sure. The memory has been distorted by years. Perhaps I surrendered knowing he was going to catch me. Perhaps I wanted to be caught. But I screamed "NO!" as he grabbed me from behind and covered my mouth with his dirty hand. He stuck his other hand down my shorts. He kept it there even as I peed myself. Then he shoved me down hard and yelled, "Now go!" I caught up with my crying friend. We stumbled to the top of the ravine road. A police car was parked there. We didn't ask for help. They might well have caught him but we didn't trust the cops. We thought we'd get in trouble. I ended up sitting in the principal's office with two plainclothes officers. I answered their questions. It wasn't in my vocabulary to describe a man jacking off. "His zipper was… open," was all I could say. Later I learned the school authorities thought it best to downplay the incident for my sake. I just remember wondering why all these adults were acting as though nothing had happened. Sometime later I was brought to the courthouse to identify spect in a line-up. I agreed to it as long as I didn't have to see him. was taken into a big room full of all kinds of people. It was terrifying. I kept looking for the two-way mirror. There wasn't one. A man with curly black hair was staring at me. I identified him. I was wrong. He was a policeman. The suspect was released. Nobody was ever caught. For a long time I was ashamed of what happened. Part of me was proud. It made me special. But I learned to fear men. And intimacy. I confuse sex with love. I have this private fantasy. I'm saying no but the man doesn't stop. I get off on it. You know how much work I've done on myself? Countless fathoms. You know how I see it now? It was grace. He didn't drag me into the woods and leave me dead in the mud. He let me go.

"Micheline"
from

All Other Destinations are Cancelled
Colleen Murphy

Micheline, age seventeen to twenty, is a small-town prostitute. She tells her mother how her father once tried to shoot her.

MICHELINE

I was just followin' the tracks. Could barely make them out, and Dad was walkin' behind me, CREEPIN' behind me sayin', "Keep goin' Mitch, keep goin." And I didn't even wanna shoot a stupid moose, but he kept shoutin' "Look down Mitch, keep watchin those tracks" Talkin' to me like I was Touser, 'member Touser? That mongrel we had and when it got sick Dad wouldn't get it gassed cause he said the dog would SMELL what was gonna happen. So instead Dad took a piece of moose meat outta the freezer, put his gun in the trunk, Touser in the back seat and drove out to Dead Otter Creek? 'Member? Took the dog out into the middle of the bush and gave him the steak, and Touser, he musta been all excited chompin' away at the meat when Dad lines up his 308 against Touser's ear. Said the dog didn't even know what hit him… but dogs aren't that dumb, and you know what? I started to feel like Touser, smellin' Dad's stinky aftershave and that's when I turned around and there he was friggin' holdin' his gun up lookin' at me through the sights an' I screamed, "DAD!" He says in a really calm voice, "Don't call me Dad", then KA-POW and… he missed! So I, I started runnin' through the bush, branches were hittin' me, I was trippin' over stumps, slippin' into the water, my feet soaked an' hearin' those shots PING PING ricochetin' offa trees, runnin', shit—my heart fallin' outta my lungs, and then I see this bone lyin' on the ground an' it's— I don't know, I don't know what I was thinking—I just GRABBED IT and stumbled out onto the highway. I didn't know if he was lost or hidin' behind a tree AIMIN' at me while I stood there an' I STOOD, hopin',

...ayin', but not one single measly lousy car comes by. After a while I didn't feel anything anymore, just stood holdin' this, I don't know what it was—looked like a piece of Touser's leg or somethin'. Then I hear him. "Mitch? Where are you? We gotta go home now." So we went home.

from

Mother Tongue
Betty Quan

— ◎ — ◎ —

MIMI

Sometimes when I dream, I dream in Chinese. Not the pidgin
Chinese I've developed but the fluent, flowing language my father used
to coo as he walked with me, hand in hand. There is this one dream. I am
walking with my father in the alleyway behind our house. I am seven years
old. This is just before my father... before.... My father and I are holding
hands and in perfect Cantonese talk about the snow peas in the garden that
are ready for picking. Father doesn't know it, but for the past week I've
been hiding amongst the staked vines, in the green light, gorging on the
snow peas until there can't be any more left. I'm about to tell him this—air
my confession—when we come across a large kitchen table propped against
the side of the garage. "A race, my little *jingwei*" my Father says. "I'll go
through the tunnel and we'll see which way is faster. One, two, three,
GO!" We run; him in the tunnel, me on the gravel. I finish first and wait,
expecting to meet him and rejoin hands. But he doesn't come out of the
shadows. My extended hand is empty. I wait and wait and wait. I start
screaming, *(in Chinese)* "Father! Father! Come back! Please come back!
Father!" *(in English)* And then, I wake up.

"Barry Sim"
from

Memory Tours: an interactive play
Emma Roberts

Lill returns to the town she grew up in after many years of travelling. The book in question is an antique copy of *Jane Eyre*, one of six items that she has kept in a fireproof box. She passes each item to the audience and then tells the story behind it, as it is passed from person to person.

LILL

There is an antique book in my collection, an ancient copy of *Jane Eyre*. It is no larger than my hand and it smells like two hundred years. It's one of my most cherished possessions.

The inscription reads: "With love, from Uncle Barry & Auntie Bar, Feb. 1980"

My dad got a job in the credit department of a small drapery manufacturer, in the early eighties. Uncle Barry was Barry Sim, the interior decorator who ran the in-house showroom. Auntie Bar, a.k.a Margaret Sim, was his wife. My dad and Barry struck up a friendship, somehow. Barry referred to my father as "worldly," and "civilised," and Barry was the type of man for whom these attributes were important: they distinguished the cultured man from the mangy pack. Barry appeared in a different suit every day, complete with cufflinks, tie clip, polished shoes, and clean, immaculate hands. He spent his days in the showroom, creating displays that perhaps a half-dozen people would see, but they were perfect: the colours exquisitely and expertly matched. My mother and I were never sure how or why these two became friends: my dad said Barry reminded him of the finer things in life.

We began to spend more time with the Sims. They would invite us over for dinner, and afterwards, Barry would show my dad his collection of antiques. This is when I realised the essence of their friendship. My father's eyes would gleam when Barry would show us the tea set from Henry VIII, the Chinese paintings from a dynasty long dust, the mahogany sideboard that had served the previous century. The Sims' house was a treasure trove of time.

I, on the other hand, spent most of my time with Margaret. She was the most elegant woman I had ever seen. She was extremely tall and thin, with a coil of white hair, a willowy neck and a smoky, Connecticut voice that seemed steeped in money. I can't explain that voice. In hindsight, I can only say it was one of privilege: a voice that came from someone who never questioned the feasibility of anything. Margaret was someone who never needed luck. Auntie Bar always wore dresses and high-heeled shoes, even though she spent most of her time at home, and carefully prepared lunches for me on plates so pretty that I was too scared to eat from them. She made a grape juice punch with cinnamon sticks and made me a dolly out of blue yarn. She and Barry didn't have any children.

After my parents split up, we all went our separate ways, and as is typical of these family implosions, the friends that I had grown up with ceased to exist. I moved into a new city and a new realm.

And then, I moved back.

When you return to a town that you've spent more than ten years in, so that you know every blade of grass by name, it is rare to find things similar to what you recall. There is a certain pervasive disillusionment that occurs, once you crack the seal on your memory. Everything is smaller, shabbier, the people are older and they don't seem quite so smart. There are new buildings everywhere, and a lot of the old ones are down. The river is dirtier, the highway is wider, and the cinemas you longed for as a child are finally open, but it's meaningless now. The boy you fell in love with in grade ten is dead. You can go see his grave on the top of the hill. But you don't.

So, here I was, after several years away. Nothing had changed. Except for me. I got a job as a waitress in a roadside "roadhouse," a tired little dive on the outskirts of town. I was often the only female, there was never a mixed drink to be served, and the tips averaged about three percent. Across the street, the famous "No Tell Motel" loomed. I never once called it by its real name. It was likely "Shady Lanes" or "Maple Grove" or some damn ridiculous thing: not one shrub sat within a mile of this sad long centipede of a building, full of broken-down folks on their last legs.

It was August. They were ripping up one of the lanes of the road between the bar and the motel. All of us were moving slug-like under a crushing sun, especially the road works guys. I was on afternoons, pissed off, since this was the worst shift for money and the other waitress had called in sick. The only excitement was when one of the workers stumbled in bleeding sweat and panting for beer. But, on this day, none of them were cute, and all of them were old. I was standing behind the bar when an old man in a suit walked in by himself. He sat at a table in the opposite section.

As I neared his table, a whoosh of recognition flew through my head and clattered like a stone in my stomach. I thought, "Jesus Christ, that's Barry."

I had heard from my mother that Margaret had died. Barry hadn't taken it well, was all I knew. The specifics were withheld. But, I felt someone push the past up behind me: it landed with a soft little thud in the small of my back.

Barry was still in a suit, yes, but it wasn't so clean. He was missing a cufflink. There was a strange bloated puffiness lingering around his face and neck. He looked directly at me and said,

"Could I have a Bloody Mary, please?"

The last time my mother had seen Barry, before his house inexplicably went up for sale, he was hungover and throwing up in the hydrangea bush. She said it was the worst afternoon of her life. She kept hearing Margaret's ghost weeping. But what could she do?

As a child there had been the simple observation that when Dad had beer, Barry had club soda and lemon, and when Dad had a brandy, Barry had a cup of tea. That was it. I was never told in plain terms.

I went back behind the bar and spent ten minutes building the Bloody Mary. I was thinking of the tea set from Henry VIII, making sure I didn't disappoint Uncle Barry. I was thinking, "Imagine when he realises it's me!"

I brought it over on the tray and set it down before him. I waited, smiling. Barry looked up at me and said, "Thank you."

I returned to the bar and then another table came in. At that same moment, I heard, "Miss! Miss!" from Barry's corner of the room.

As I approached him the second time, I saw that he had upended the Bloody Mary all over himself. I grabbed a handful of napkins from the basket and returned. I leaned over to help him with the spill, and as I stood there, so close to him, I imagined myself saying, "It's me, Uncle Barry. Don't you remember?" I looked at him again. There was absolutely no recognition in his eyes. There was nothing in his eyes. It wasn't that they were dead either. They were pickled. I saw then, that Uncle Barry was absolutely, positively blotto.

He asked for the bill. I brought it. I didn't wait for him to pay me. He left ten dollars on the table and staggered out. It was a decent tip. I picked up the napkin, thinking he might have left me a note. There was only tomato juice. I looked out the window, then. I wish I hadn't. Barry was attempting to cross the road, in the middle of the construction, listing heavily, paying too much attention to standing upright and not enough to staying out of traffic. I saw him lurch through the work site, translucent waves of heat floating up from the asphalt, the dust engulfing him; one of the workers snarled something at him, another pushed him gently towards the motel.

And indeed, that's where he was, Room Six at the Twilight Pines or whatever the hell it was called. I watched the door close behind him.

I threw the lemon from the Bloody Mary into the sink.

I still have the *Jane Eyre* book, here with me on my bookshelf. The dolly has long since disappeared, and I never wrote down the recipe for the grape juice punch. I do think of Barry, now and then, mostly when I'm marvelling at how people change, but sometimes, when I'm sitting in a bar, watching the old men drink, and stare, alone.

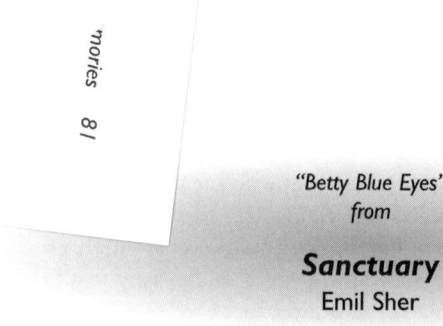

"Betty Blue Eyes"
from

Sanctuary
Emil Sher

Every week, June—an emotionally abused woman—retreats to a secluded spot in a park for some time alone. For a year, Philip has watched her from a distance. He introduces himself on the very morning when June has come to scatter her husband's ashes. June asks Philip if he has ever seen anyone burn, then recounts the memory of a childhood doll.

JUNE

Betty. Her name was Betty. Betty with the beautiful eyes. Blue, blue, blue. Long, dark lashes. Soft, blonde hair. Didn't weigh more than a pound. *(beat)* My absolute favourite doll. Barbie was too bony. Her tits scared me. And I never trusted Ken. Too perfect. But Betty was mine. *(pause)* I can't remember exactly what it was I'd done, but I'd done something to make my mother angry. Really angry. She must've been having a hard day. Yeah, I'm sure she was just having one of those days. I was about five, maybe six. I probably did what every five-year-old does at one time or another, something that makes a parent's eyes turn funny. I said I was sorry. But that wasn't good enough. "That's not good enough, young lady." My mother must have told me that about a thousand times. Do you know what happens to young girls who misbehave? That's when she did it. I begged her not to, but she wouldn't have any of it. She plops Betty onto a tray and throws her into the oven. Soon there's this awful smell filling the kitchen. I stood there, practically blind for all the tears in my eyes. My mother walks in every ten minutes to check on Betty. "Look, June. Look what's happening to Betty." And she made me look, making me promise I'd always behave. Betty's arms and legs were melting, melting and her hair was sizzling. On it went, 'til there was nothing left but a puddle of Betty, and two blue eyes.

from

The Flower of the Flock
Irene N. Watts

1980. Lily Ransome finally discloses her past to her daughter. The living room of Lily's home. She is sorting through her possessions.

— ◎ — ◎ —

LILY

      I was born in Stepney, London. All I remember of the house was the kitchen full of steam, water running down the walls in steady drops. Mother took in washing. Father had left home when I was born. One morning, I must've been five or six years old, mother said, "we're going out." That didn't happen often. She took my hand in her chapped calloused one. After a long time walking, we stopped in front of a big gloomy house. It gave me shivers. Mother rang the bell and a woman opened the door. Black dress, white apron. The staircase behind her went up and up, into the sky, I thought. The floor was so shiny you could see your face in it. Mother said, "'er name's Lily. Lily Ransome. Take 'er please, I can't manage no more." She kissed my cheek then and said, "mind your manners Lil, I'll be back for you if I can." And that's how I came to be a Barnardo's girl: "No destitute child ever refused admission."

We got to wear a uniform and shoes that fit most of the time. We ate regular—three meals a day, soup and bread and tea. At Christmas we got an orange. We worked hard, who do you think polished those floors? But I learned to read and write and slept in a bed with clean sheets.

One day us big girls—the ones who were nine and over, were called into the dining hall. That was in 1913. A man told us we were "The flower of the flock, Little Empire Builders." He said the Canadians are waiting to take us into their homes. Good homes, where they'd treat us like family. There'd be horses to ride, and snow to play in. They said my mother had gone to heaven. I don't know if it was true. We sailed across the ocean on the *Sicilian*. I never forgot my first sight of Halifax harbour. I thought I'd die happy if I could live by the sea and taste the salt spray on my lips, and hear the cry of the gulls as they swooped so free in the sky. They put us on a train to Peterborough, Ontario. I just wanted to stop moving. I was found a place on a farm. I was ten. I washed a lot of floors and scrubbed a lot of kids. I learned to milk cows, they were company. One winter it was so cold, my hands froze to the pump. I waited for a kind word, for someone to call me Lily instead of "you" or "girl." That's all I ever was to them, "The Home Girl." I never once ate with the family, or had time to go to school. I left when I was fourteen, they wouldn't pay me wages. I went into service. This is the first dollar I ever earned. I swore I'd never spend it. I never told anyone I was a Home girl. Your father didn't even know.

He was lost at sea in World War II. Why did they send us away, to give us a better life or because we were cheap labour?… I'd have liked to have seen my mother one more time.

IDENTITY

"Carrie" by Nina Aquino
from

Miss Orient(ed)

Aquino and Nadine Villasin

Carrie, a beauty pageant contestant of "Miss Pearl of the Orient," privately recalls the pivotal moment she decided to become a true Canadian.

CARRIE

L'Oreal Feria Champagne Cocktail, number 91. Doesn't it look pretty? Twenty-two dollars and eighty-five cents, six hundred Shoppers Drug Mart Optimum points. The lady behind the counter asks me if I want to redeem my already thirteen thousand points and get fifty-five percent off of my box of hair colour.

"No thank you," I tell her.

She looks up from the counter and notices me for the first time.

"Oh," she utters.

"What?"

"It's not going to work."

"What's not going to work?"

"This colour…" and she points to the box of my precious hair dye.

"You need to strip your hair…you know…strip the black out of it."

"I didn't know you had to do that," I say.

"Yeah well, I used to work at a salon…I've seen how they do it."

She then proceeds to grab a chunk of my hair and starts rubbing it between her fingers… this lady—this old, ugly, crusty-looking Shoppers Drug Mart lady, with her blue-and-red striped uniform, mascara-laden eyelashes, her brown roots peeking out of her tacky Clairol Desert Sunrise, number 15, 6.99 dyed hair—is touching my hair!

"Yep," she says. "No matter how much of this blonde gunk you put in your hair, it's going to remain black."

I must have looked disappointed or something 'coz she immediately followed it up with "it's not your fault sweetie... you can't help it... it's the kind of hair you have... you know..."

"No, I don't know." I tell her.

"The new colour will slip right off. You're not going to look like this..." and she picks up the box and suddenly... I see myself face to face with the woman on the box... her soft brown eyes, her Aphrodite nose... full red lips... and the hair... the luscious, luscious, blonde hair.

Great...humiliated, sized-up and hair molested by a fucking Shoppers Drug Mart lady. Who the fuck does she think she is?

But I look at the box again... and the beautiful woman... the eyes... the lips... the nose... and the hair... the luscious, luscious blonde hair... God, if I can't have the eyes, the nose and the lips... at least let me have the hair... please let me have the hair.

And this fucking Shoppers Drug Mart lady knows how to do it... she knows how to make my hair blonde and pretty... she knows how to make me pretty... you know... pretty as a Canadian, prettier than a Filipino...

"So, do you want your hair to look like this or not?"

No choice... I need her... Champagne Cocktail, number 91.

"Listen Miss... Miss..."

"What do I have to do?"

She smiles, quickly makes her way out of the counter and grabs my arm.

"I thought you'd never ask... follow me honey." Like a prophet leading its disciple to salvation, she guides me towards the "Hair Care" aisle and well... *(points to her newly dyed hair)*

Doesn't it look pretty?

Well, doesn't it?

Awkward silence. Beat.

Damn... I should've just redeemed those bloody points.

from

Buzzcut

Maja Ardal

A small hair salon in a rural village. It is a storefront. Inside the decor is from the fifties. Pale pink walls, and placards of models sporting very traditional hair styles. There is a price list on the wall, one chair for the customer, and one mirror. A trolley loaded with jumbo rollers, perming rollers, hair spray, and other paraphernalia. Under the mirror is a large jar with blue liquid, and a bouquet of tail combs.

Corrina is in her late forties. Lots of make-up, and thick around the middle. She wears a pink old-fashioned smock, and under it, stretch leggings, and flashy-looking mules on her feet. She is sitting in a hairdressing chair leafing through a magazine. She sees Alice peering in through the window

CORRINA

Come on in. You looking for a cut? I'll do ya. I was just taking a break on account of my legs. Thirty years of this and I've varicose veins the size of snakes. Have a seat. Price list's in front of ya. You want a perm, colour job, a nice set of bangs, straight as a ruler, I'm your gal. *(starts to set up combs and scissors)* Oh, I'm not saying I only do one style, though. I'll do your Farrah Fawcett look—that's mainly for weddings and graduations—and that needs a *lot* of know-how. A lot more'n you think. First, it's all in the cut. That'll take about half an hour to do it right. Then another half-hour with the big roller brush and the hair dryer, to flick the front back like wings. Take a seat. Some hair can't take it. The soft fine hair, the kind that sits flat on their heads after a wash. Well, that's when the spray comes in. Gel won't do it. It's got to be a nice hard-rock spray, that'll keep the wing bits up from the morning till the party's over. *(puts the cape around ALICE)* I've seen girls out back of the dances, who've had too many daiquiris, their dresses all mussed up, their eye make-up down to their chins, puking their guts up, and every flicked-back hair is still in place. I'll say to myself, "That's a Corrina's Cut'n Curl hair-do." That gives me a bit of pride. I won't deny it.

(holds up magazine) See these pictures? These Millenium models? See this hair sticking up in all directions, every jeezdarn hair cut a different length? That's nothing more than bed-head. It's the "I've gone off my nut" look! Won't last, though. I'm not going to some special training in the city just so's I can make your hair look like you're in the mental hospital. See their eyes? They look like kids who've been on the streets all their life. They put the eyeshadow *under* the eyes. Know what they call it? It's written right here... Heroin chick! And their faces are more like skulls. I don't care how the jeez much these girls make, and I know it's a—*lot!* One of my customers told me that they starve themselves if they want to make it to the top. Starve yourself, put shadow under your eyes, and pull your hair in every direction, and you'll get your face in *Vogue*, 'cos you look like a drug addict, and that sells clothes and hair-dos! Puts me off my lunch. If anyone came in here and asked for that look, I'd say, "Go see a doctor".

(observes ALICE's hair) Oh geez! I don't piss on the competition, but the last person who cut you should be run out of town. And your colour's wrong for your eyes, dear. You want to hide the grey, you do it with a nice shiny copper, not that yellow streaky thing. See now it looks like you got sun damage, and tried to cover it up. You need a nice natural colour like burnished copper. Put a glow on your skin. I use it on every lady in this town over forty. No one's complained yet. I want to be able to look my customers in the eyes when they come in. Oh, take your time. I don't want to rush you. *(opens a magazine)* See? That's the colour I'm talking about. I keep the old magazines around for people your age. No buzzcuts in this salon... I like my ladies happy.

Can you imagine if I screwed up? I'd have to look at that cut every time I go to the Legion, or the Corner Mart. Every time I go to church, I have to sit behind a row of *my* heads. I tell you, It's hard to focus on the sermon when I see a head that should've come in a month ago, or hair that someone tried to cut themselves. *(starts to feel ALICE's hair)* One time I got so mad, I took out my mini-spray, and fixed the curls back of Barb MacDonald's head during the prayer. She'd tried to twist it up, like I'd done for her son's wedding, and it was an unholy mess. The coils were all sprung loose, and dangling and bouncing all over the back of her neck. I thought

I'd blow a fuse, so when she bowed her head, for the prayer, I thought, okay, everyone's got their eyes closed. Now's my chance. I took out my tail comb—I always keep a tail comb handy—and I pressed each coil into place, real careful, then I took out my mini hairspray, and gave the whole back of her head a long spray. Good as glue. Well, all you heard in that place was a loud hiss. But you know the power of the church. Nobody dares to make a fuss when they're talking to God, not even Barb.

When she came outside I heard her telling the Father that she'd heard God breathing into her ear during the prayer. She had a spiritual awakening. She stopped drinking that very day, and I'm responsible. And I didn't charge her a dime. So. What's it to be?

from

Bitter Rose
Catherine Banks

Rose (forty-three) is the mother of two, a wife and an artist without a body of work. On this ordinary day Rose got up, put on her wedding dress, smeared it with red paint (blood) and went off to do her regular errands. Now barricaded in the family rec room she is very close to facing what not working has cost her.

ROSE

     When all this began, this metaphoric thing, I bought a bikini. I wear it strictly for the tan lines, which I find funny and sexy at the same time. I stand in the mirror and grin at my body; all my exciting bits *exposed in gleaming white.*

When I was a girl of ten I skinned rabbits. Every second day in winter I would follow my brother into the woods to check our snares. Often there were the stiff frozen corpses, laid out as though still in the act of running. Once in my snare, we found one newly caught. I cried until my brother killed it with his hands because the noose was already too tightly drawn and I didn't want to leave it. For once knowing exactly the suffering I inflicted.

Later in the sour cellar, the rabbit hung by its back legs, I cut precisely so as not to damage the coat. I peeled back its skin inch by inch, exposing its blue flesh, veined in purple, gleaming maps to the terrible vulnerability of its soft body.

     ROSE pauses hugging her own body.

I recently read the saddest story in the world. No, not the saddest, the most harrowing. After I read it I went to bed and cried. I had to go to bed even though it was arsenic hour, even though I had 15 minutes to get supper on the table and 29 minutes to get Margaret to Brownies and Susan to piano.

An artist, a man of great talent and influence, described how one night at a launching of a book of his work he noticed a middle-aged woman watching him from a little distance away and even though several times there clearly was an opening for her to come forward and have her copy signed, she did not. Finally, when the room was almost cleared and even he had begun to get ready to leave, *she propelled herself forward as if toward her own death.*

Excuse me, she said, *I want to ask you, when you are an artist and you don't have any work… what I mean is you haven't created a body of work yet, how do you call yourself an* artist?

Oh my God.

The great artist gave a very kind and helpful answer… but for days I've been caught prisoner in that place where she is just about to be propelled forward.

Did he have to say *middle-aged?* Did he have to write, *as if propelled towards her own death?* Did he have to write down those words, *how do you call yourself an artist without a body of work?*

Did he have to peel back my skin inch by inch by inch?

"imogene"
from

yagayah
naila belvett and d'bi.young

mary is in kingston, jamaica, summertime in 1993. imogene is in montreal, canada, winter 1993.

imogene

canada...

why is your accent so thick? how come you can't speak proper english? you don't speak french... where do you come from? here i am an immigrant inna foreign land. in jamaica i was imogene, mass edwards dawta... here i am just black, black and struggling... and they hate jamaicans. every crime weh commit is a jamaican get blame fi it. every black person is a jamaican as far as dese people are concerned. african, trinidadian, vincencian, guyanese, all of us are "jamaican" here. first they say we come an take away their jobs, then they say that we are all on welfare. mi sey—di white people don't want us in dem land. and it's not even their land cause dem tief it from the indian people dem. basically my father and i are struggling here mary. he—well, he just lost his job and they are telling him that he has to go back to school even though he studied mechanical engineering in jamaica for so many years. they told me that i have to redo a couple of years of high school cause dem have one different school system here. as a result i decided to take some time off from school so that i could work. but i am going to night school instead. right now i have a telemarketing job cause work over here is hard to get. if i don't work we won't be able to pay the rent. if you can't pay rent then you're "ass out" as they say here.

mi seh mary, please don't believe them when they say that there are no poor people in foreign. people sleep pon di streets here just like they do inna jamdown. but at least inna jamaica there is an excuse for the poverty, mi wan know a wha kind of excuse they have here—first-world country mi ras.

ah telling yuh mary, dese people don't mix with black people much. they have their own neighbourhoods wid big house and car and plenty lan. one rich neighbourhood name westmount is right beside one poor neighbourhood name st. henri.

mary foreign is not easy. i know that jamaica is hard but when you come here is a new set of battles. i will try to send you a pair of shoes and a brief fi jacob as soon as i work some money.

your friend, imogene

from

Serviced
Tony Berto

Roz is a well seasoned, aggressive waiter; Terry, a neophyte in the same popular, but run-down watering hole. Immediately before this monologue, Roz has caught a customer stepping out of line. As she is about to intervene and discipline and such, Terry asks her "isn't the customer always right?" While she displays bravado, there ought also to be—in the monologue—an element of her psyching herself up to go into battle.

ROZ

No, nay, never, not. Not in this place. The customer is not always right. *(cuts TERRY off)* Now, that's what we call interrupting. *(holds up a finger)* "Why?" Terry, you were gonna ask? Cause we're booze. We're booze oriented. We're a bar. In case you haven't noticed, it's my job to take charge around here. Ever since some jerk got drunk and killed a model Christian family and then sued the bar that got him drunk—we've been pooched. The goddamn government and the courts have decided that, as boozemeister, *I* am ultimately responsible for the fate of whatever skid I get drunk. Some slug wants to go get in a car after I served him and run over a row of nuns in wheelchairs, well, then *I* get sued. So, it's my job to get 'em pissed but keep 'em in line.

…I've already told that asswipe three times…

And so, in the bar business, therefore, I'm always right. The customer is always wrong. By the way, this beer just leapt out of the fridge at me. I marked it on your spill sheet. *(clandestinely pounds a beer)*

And so of course I can cut whomever off, whenever, and do, if the whim strikes me. Hence the need for bouncers, or in our case, my partial role as a gorgon…

(again thwarts an interruption) I perhaps can understand your confusion my friend but never, ever, doubt my power. Just because places like the Black Hole are performing anthropological experiments with proto-humanoids and like to label them "security staff" does not mean that our enlightened—some might say over-enlightened—twenty-first century model here *(uses a Vanna White pose on herself)* is not a bouncer.

How do I look, would you be scared? *(exits)*

"Holes"
from

Provenance
Ronnie Burkett

LEDA

There are holes in my shoes
That's provenance, dears
Age-hardened leather grows thin through the years
For too many dances
Blister the soul
And covering your tracks in the dirt takes its toll
How droll, I admit
Counterfeit, a fraud on the stroll
I've traded the past, squandered my history
Always well-heeled but shrouded in mystery
With no one to know me, no one will miss me
Oh dear
No, running's my best-suited role

There are holes in my heart
This provenance, alone
A beating, bloodless fist chewed to the bone
Bludgeoned but not beaten
Buried alive
Pounding bloody marvel willed to survive
Revive, it dares me
It wears me and won't be deprived
My heart isn't true, but one truth I've known
Red goes with everything, blue's best alone
Heart on wing, the ugly cygnet has flown
So alone
No, this is my secret swan dive

There are holes in the story
This provenance, mine
Gaps in the journey forgotten with time
Beginnings unfinished
Endings not met
Bushels of middles I choose to forget
And yet, I cannot
I forgot to bury regret
I've dampened the laughter, dried all my tears
Smothered the gasping for breath through the years
Danced with the devil, and still I am here
It's mine
No, this is the version you get

from

Ruf Paradise
Alec Butler

— ⊚ — ⊚ —

The only time I saw my dad cry was when I got home that night.
He's sitting at the kitchen table, just about to leave for the graveyard shift,
I had just come back from walking Darla home.
He knows where I've been and who with.
"Stay away from that girl, she's putting ideas in your head."
"Nobody's putting ideas in my head," I shot back.
"Don't get smart with me young lady.
I just finished telling your mother I'm getting laid off next week.
Now I get a call from that girl's mother, yellin' that my daughter
Should be shipped off to the Butterscotch Palace.
You start wearing dresses, tomorrow."
"Fuck you, Dad."
Dad's pissed, he grabs me and tries to pull down my pants.
"You're still young enough to take over my knee, young lady"
Next thing I know, I'm down on the kitchen floor.
He pulls back in shock…
I'm wearing a pair of my brother's briefs with a pair of workingman's socks
shoved down the front.
I can't see Dad's tears because his face is buried in his hands.
"Where's my daughter?" he's weeping over and over, "where's my
daughter?"

I can't change what Dad did.
I had to go to a bigger place.
Out of the shadows of the steel plant,
Out from under the thumb of people who wanted me to be like them.
So the next summer I stuck out my thumb and hitched a ride to the City of
Dreams beyond the City on the other side of the Overpass.
I found my community of freaks.

For years I lived as a butch, learning the ropes about life and art
Learning how to survive the streets from drag queens and sex workers.
Taking my cues about how to dress from
old-school working-class bull daggers at the Chez.
Things I didn't learn in the Funk & Wagnall's.

But there was something missing.
While taking care of a couple of friends with AIDS.
I was so busy I never had time to shave.
One day my beard was so obvious, I was clipping Michael's toenails
and he calls me a "beautiful daddy bear."
The next day I'm giving Kevin a bath, he sez to me
"you're some handsome woman, man, whatever you are."
Nobody had ever called me handsome or beautiful before.
After they died a week apart, I stopped shaving altogether.
But I didn't expect other people, people who called themselves freaks,
to cross to the other side of the street when they saw me coming.
I wondered if another woman would ever touch me again.
Now I was an outsider among outsiders.

Later some of those same sisters
Started growing beards of their own and calling me "brother"
Some offer to "fix" me, like the doctors back home.
"Deepen your voice or you won't pass."
"Look at the size of your breasts, man, what will people think?"
But my story does not belong to them.
I do not want to become a guy just like the guys
who wanted to kill me when I was fourteen.
I wonder when my new brothers shake my hand, slap my back and
welcome me are they seeing what they want to see?
Looking back I ask myself if anyone ever really saw me?
Then I remember the angels who did.
Ma, my champion. Darla, my first crush.
Kathleen, my dyke mentor. Leanne, my little girl.
Michelle, my fallen queen.
Thru their love I learned to love myself in all my aspects.
Tomboy, artist, writer
drag king, butch dyke, beatnik
daddy, bear, Two-Spirited,
freak.

"*Grace*"
from

Marrying Frame
John Frizzell

Blocky, manicured, Grace, tumbles through the nicotine-glazed clutter of her ranch-style back-split, and flops onto the misshapen sofa. Her purchases scatter. The sofa is still depressed from her late husband, Frame, as is she. Grace wrestles off her weary fur, pops a couple of dolls, and sparks a Pall Mall. She scans the hapless furnishings, most of which Frame, an enthusiastic, talent-free carpenter, cobbled together.

Grace yanks a tangled garland from a Supersave bag. She jams and pokes the cheap tinsel around the jumble on the mantelpiece. A yank at the fancy foil-iage, a grim Fa-la-la-la, and one of the mantle's three figurines is inadvertently knocked to the Palos Verdes tile below. After gazing balefully at the shards, Grace finally acknowledges the audience…

GRACE

   I'm sorry. I bet it was your favorite. It was, wasn't it? "Top O'the Hill." If Frame were alive I'd be hearing about it for a month of Sundays. Years of meticulous estate planning shot to hell. *(imitates Frame)* "Three girls, three figurines, Grace. Get it? Hel-lo?!"

   Like a docent, GRACE introduces each object.

Leading Lady, goes to Diana. Dee did *Annie Get your Gun* at L.C. Venetian Ball is Kim's because Halloween was her big thing then. Top O'the Hill, …well, mostly it was me liked it. Jenny'd wanted GIC's but Frame said these were better investments. Frame never had a real grip on finances. He was picking up Beanie Babies at the end. Oh he was fortune's fool, that one. Which is a stick Jenny loves poking me with. Though why I should be piqued by his lack of financial acumen beats me. Particularly given her husband is such an obsequious clown. Mind you, she's safe knowing I'll never throw it back at her. Mothers and daughters don't play on a level field. Anyway, much as she professed hating Top O The Hill, she'll notice she's gone the moment she steps in. And I don't know why, but I'm going to lie. Obviously I could say I knocked it off, it's reasonable. Things happen. But I won't, I'm unable to reveal even my minor mistakes to her. None too maternal I know, but I'm competitive with her. And I value things I've learned I am.

She won't care about the figurine, but we were all so tyrannised by Frame's insistence on keeping it all equal, she'll manage a little panic. He was so damn picky. Dollars to donuts he's turning heaven upside down right now looking for the crazy glue.

She tosses the larger pieces into the fireplace, then perches on an arm of the out-scale sofa.

I was so sure if I got married it'd all be fine. Frame Keller's wife. Mrs. Keller. The Kellers. "Grace and Frame Keller." "Let freedom ring"—I had it all thought out. We'd cut coupons, and scrimp and save to be snowbirds when he retired. That would pass as our style, it would explain things we didn't have, or wouldn't do. Anything we did do, we'd consider a splurge, and naughty. So fun was built right in. We'd drive second-hand cars, but always a luxury model, the Marquis Brougham, or Monterrey. We'd play euchre Wednesdays with Frank and Vera Holland, though everyone would know I didn't care for it. I saw us as putterers. We wouldn't be into TV, but we wouldn't be readers either. We'd garden, but wouldn't be gardeners. We'd cook, but wouldn't be cooks. We'd putter. I'd yo-yo diet, talk about taking night courses, and soon be too fat to keep pretending I enjoyed the sex thing. We'd ape opinions from talk radio, and say angry uninformed things about politics. I saw Grace Keller so clearly.

But I'll tell you how I made the mistake. Frame was bald by 23, and wore wacky suspenders, bright "look at me" suspenders. A whole collection. So naturally I mistakenly assumed he had personality.

Christ on a muffin! That was the deal, that was him. I married a suspender collection, "Do you take this comic substitution for a belt to be your lawfully wedded…"

She sprawls on the sofa, throwing her leg akimbo over the back cushion, and stares up.

What I'd do to go back and be born some huge, wild, lesbian, you know, or a Siamese twin, something along that order. Something fun. Concrete. Who knows what she thinks, what she wears, what she wants for dinner. Everything clear. Everything laid out. Wouldn't you kill to be Helen Keller, or a Quint?

I do not blame God though. Oh no. I blame that Mary. God's busy, and probably doesn't really give a shit. Mary though? That kind of woman always picks my ass. And vice a versa. A lot of it's her fault, I don't know how I know, I just do. Trust me.

The day Jenny was born was the most exciting ever. Total buzz. Sure beat anything I ever smoked or swallowed, no contest. Not because of birth, or anything like that. Well, partly. I was the moment I realised and accepted I didn't like the girl. Cranky little baby. Not one smidge. The whole show gave me creeps. From Frame's greasy sperm climbing up there, then that fetus growing in me... ucch, women saying I'd fall head over heels in love with it. Hardly. But for the first time I felt a little real, a bit unique. And it felt pretty damn good, boy. Jenny caught on of course, wouldn't breastfeed. Screamed, or clammed up. Till she got teeth, then she went at me with a vengeance. Like a lamprey. Been like that between us ever since. Of course it makes her snaky—our little war—feeds me. Watch, she'll prance in here with a box of chocolates, or something nice from duty free. All sweet and affectionate, "what's past is past." Butter wouldn't melt—all of it just to scare the shit out of me. I'm serious. It'll work too.

But she can't keep it up. Starts bugging her when I don't ask about the kids. If she jumps the gun, and tells me something, I make her repeat it. You know how you have to work hard to remember stuff that isn't important? Like that? It's cruel, okay, but this old lady's not got much left.

Dangerous game though. Watching your daughter fighting for her children makes you want to like her. Fortunately she's got Frame's porcine mug. So unsympathetic. And the shrill voice. Truly a curse.

> *GRACE tugs a little hard on her cig and begins hacking.*

Fuck me, these are foul. Been smoking over three whole weeks, near four. Damn things still make me gag. But Jenny's a gym teacher, and pregnant with grandkid numero number three. Gotta show the proper disrespect. *(She laughs.)* The day her husband heard he packed a duffle and set up camp in a motel. What did she think? Okay, she got jumping jacks the first two times, and roses, and foot rubs, and lies about the beauty of stretch marks. But he's a man who had no problem being home all day. He's even weaker than her father. And better gone, than pulling an Andrea Yates in a year. I keep thinking about the ones waiting to be drowned, why not run? Stupid I suppose.

GRACE swallows two more pills, no water.

No *agua, (mock toasting the audience)* that takes skill. The skill of a bad ventriloquist, skill nevertheless.

She holds up a small blue pill.

An addict's another thing I am…. Not so special anymore. And can't always admit it yet. Still…

Okay, if the birth was best, here's worst. First dance at our wedding, "If you don't know me by now." Ironically, I'm so full of hope I leak it. Not full like a balloon, hard. Full like a bag of milk, sloppy. When Frame whispered "I completed him, and that together we were one." I went balloon hard then, and stopped leaking. Why hadn't I seen that Grace Keller wouldn't be anything anyone wanted to be. So ashamed, finally I looked up, no one was even watching. We disappeared at our own wedding. Haven't been seen, or heard of since.

She smiles.

But Jenny is coming. Bringing gifts, like the wise men. Following the right star I hope. I really really do hope.

"Tulips"
Laurie Fyffe

A woman's struggle to survive depression, loss and disappointment in love, by finding inspiration in the beauty and resilience of a remarkable flower.

WOMAN

Pale yellows, cream tipped; hot brooding reds, deep presumptuous purples; I see entire fields, miles and miles of tulips. Their graceful cups bending ever so slightly to the warm caress of a soft breeze, or tilting coquettishly to the constant click and whir of cameras. My knees weaken, my mouth waters.

I fell in love with the tulip, at the bottom of the pit. In the hungry maw of that all-consuming slack-jawed predator, depression.

I was in another body. Reliving the last gasps of a self-inflicted demise. My friend drowned herself. Naked, dove into frigid water, and sank. And in the long nights after, I lay awake, sinking into that same coldness, sinking, a body of lead that will not rise.

> There is in God, some say
> A deep, but dazzling darkness,
> That men who cannot see, declare untrue.
> Oh, for that night, my journey to begin,
> In God to dwell, invisible and dim [1]

Imagine… a darkness that dazzles.

But I was talking about the pit. The basement of the Royal Ottawa Hospital, where I lie, slimed with Vaseline, hooked up to an ancient electrocardiogram, needle scratching.

(sings) "Serzone and Visken, will get you frisken."

Serzone and Visken, or, Diazepam, Oxazepam, Prozac, whatever, real drugs, I'm going to be on real drugs! Not the quick, sniff, puff, and snort of my youth, no these babies have stockholders, a pedigree of multi-million dollar R and D. And in their embrace I am going to sink softly, unresistingly, into the private cocoon of chemical remodification.

Then one day, pedalling from hospital to home, following that winding, narrow broken canal that meanders through this National Capital—slash—Capitale Nationale, I look up and there they are! Bed after bed of the genus *Tulipa*. And suddenly I was hooked. Lust at first linger. Why? Because the tulip is a survivor. The bulb actually withdraws underground to protect itself from extremes. Too cold? Hibernate. Too hot? Sublimate. Wait it out. Even the most passionless season can't last forever. See the world. Yes, like all survivors the tulip is a traveller. From central Asia to Europe, Spain, Holland, and now, Ottawa.

This isn't just a flower; it's a historical force to be reckoned with! In 1686 ten bulbs of the *Tulipa Semper Augustus* went for 12,000 florins. Tulip-o-mania was at its peak. A year later, the tulip crashed. People lost fortunes. It's hard to forgive a flower for that. You'd think people would make war on a piece of vegetation that caused that much grief. Off with their heads! But no! The clever tulip migrated modestly to the sturdy beds of the middle class, ensuring its survival for at least another five centuries.

My lost friend, the lady of the lake, once asked me: How long could you live without love? I should have said as long as there are tulips.

Oh, I want to shake her! I want to drag her from her weedy grave and force her to breathe deeply. Hibernate! Sublimate! Travel, God-Dammit, but live!

I love the way tulips die. A portrait of invited ravishment; petals splayed out at unnatural angles, exposing delicate protuberances, unprotected stamens trembling at the slightest vibration, before falling to earth. And, as if nature thrives on final indignities, the health of the tulip bulb is best served if the flower and leaves are left to mulch, absorbed back into the bulb to nourish the growth of another beauty, in a new season.

Now, after forty, a woman often hears the phrase; you're not old, my dear, just no longer young. Sounds an awful lot like the definition of mulch.

No! I am going to live! I am going to shoot up from the bottom of the lake! I am going to pulverise Serzone and Visken and use them for plant fertilizer. But… right now, I am going to lie down with the tulips.

Yes, as I park my bike, and in sight of Japanese tourists, madly snapping cameras, I climb into the red tulip bed. And settling into the moist earth, careful not to crush the close-packed blooms, I look up at the soft curve of these delicate, blushing underbellies and I see… yes, two lips! An eternal kiss.

There is in God a deep, but dazzling… tulip that awaits us all.

[1] *Henry Vaughan: THE NIGHT (17th century poem), Adapted.*

"Masha"
from

Walking to Russia
Jonathan Garfinkel

Masha, age nineteen, breaks free from the hospital. She tells the story of Bella. Ben is offstage.

— ◎ — ◎ —

MASHA

I heard the train go, Mama—the train is the key in the window of light— and I left that place. I escaped through the hospital door—I'm a train, Daddy, and I ride myself all the way back—AHHHHHHHH!… It's cold tonight, so cold, can't sleep, if I ever sleep they'll find me or I'll die so I keep walking… I walk straight for those tracks, turn right, and I'm gone. The stars are clear and I've never seen a moon like this before, rise above the tracks. I'm walking straight into one giant egg. Straight through that yolk and out the other side. I'm going to paint myself a home, yellow and round for my heart. My body is loose. It may as well be summer. I need to keep walking. God, you think life is this big complicated thing, really you just need to walk. I make a vow. I'll head wherever these trains go. I see the names of the towns: Pikwitonei, Ilford, Gillam, Armery, Thibaudeau. There's this magnet inside my head, pulling me further and further north. The fatigue becomes cold and I've stopped counting days. Lakes begin to freeze. Canada geese fly south. I want that love, the unbinding faith. I'm not going to stop. I follow that white prairie sun, the snow gets worse and I wear mukluks. I go farther north—brr and grrr and grr and brrr—Dusk on my left shoulder. Orion's belt above my eye. Night's so cold I sleep in my *gatkas* in the grain elevators. And the wind picks up speed there's nothing no one's gonna stop it. A thousand icicles shooting up my back and the sky is a frozen soup. I want to stick my hands in I'm so hungry I could eat the stars, one by one, little fish eggs, hmmm…. My brown fingers. I've lost my middle toe. It's always dusk. How do you explain a cold colder than cold? How do you describe the smell of ice, the breath of snow? At first you shiver, then you're numb, then you think you're gonna die. But you don't fight it, you become the cold, you enter it, its frozen bloodlines that guide you.... But now the light begins to come, each day, like a thin band of hope. And soon the snow stops. And I find creeks to drink from and eat raw Goldeye. And little shrubs begin to grow berries. And the sun is tall. It burns my eyes and it never goes down. I haven't slept in years. My feet become fire. *(lights up on Ben)* Until the tracks end. And I'm in Churchill. Polar bear capital of the world. It's just like you said, Dad, only bigger, harder than words... I keep moving. West this time. I hear the mountains. I've abandoned train tracks, there's no paths, until I reach the telegraph line. I don't know what I'm doing here. I'm dead. The world has forgotten me—Gone, bodiless. These rocks. The pale burning stone. But I keep going. I walk and I walk, it's all the thoughts burning away freezing themselves off—brrr and grr and grrr and brr—It's the necessity of movement. A want. A need. A want—*(faster)* brrr and grrr and grrr and brrr!– Until there is no more place to walk and there is only sea... brrr and grrr and grrr and brrr.... And it's the coldest winter in 300 years and I walk across that sea when it freezes—sweet Jesus walking over a thousand monsters ready to grab Him. And then land. Oh my land. I can feel it. Like nothing I have ever known. Like the land I have always known. And I can hear it: Korets. Korets. Korets. Korets.... It's the echo of snow when the winds let up. I want to go there... 5500 miles on the Trans-Siberian railway. All that cold beautiful metal, hurling its body through land, this land waking up, stretching its arms.

It's spring and the valleys' veins are coursing and the earth is in heat. The train ends in Moscow, its red spires tickle the sky, and the sun is laughing. When I arrive in Kyev I set out on horse-drawn wagon. I don't walk anymore. I take in the country. And the people's voices take me in. They eat potatoes and drink vodka, offer their daughters for marriage. And their music is this longing inside me. I want to talk to them. I wish I could ask them about the Jews, the others who lived here, for 1000 years. I arrive. Korets. But it isn't like I expected it. The houses aren't houses. They're memorials. Ruins. It's all gone: Mezeritch, Gatch, Tomashov, Kazimeirz, Dolny, Bransk...

Chelm is an industrial town and Lublin is sprawling with suburbs. I'm disappointed, Mama. I don't know what I was expecting. Some kind of solace, the warm open arms of an old baba, some chicken soup, a fiddler on the fucking roof. Where the hell do I go now? Brr and grr and grrr and brrr.... It's cold. I walk down to Grodzka Street. The stores are empty. No people in the square. A blue star. A star of David, painted on wood. Thirteenth century synagogue. I peer through the stained-glass window.

A room full of candles. Men and women, chanting beneath the golden light. I can hear it. It comes from somewhere I know. Is it inside me or out there? A community of nomads, the Lost Jews pushed to the edge of the world, with all the hope of 2000 years burning beneath the ice.

I saw his face. The man from my dream, kneeling at the *beemah*. He bowed his head and kissed his prayer book. I knew who he was. I had painted his face a thousand times. I walked inside. And his voice was sweeter than honey—Max–

I found my home. Do you hear me? Don't tell me I'm wrong. I know this crazed land and the people I love too. It's my blood, my bones, the Steppe, it's in my hair. Do you understand me? I WALKED TO RUSSIA!

"Wendy"
from

Hong Kong, Canada
Tara Goldstein

— ◎ — ◎ —

WENDY

(*stepping forward*) The day after they enrolled me at Trudeau my father and mother left Toronto to go back to Hong Kong. The last words my mother said to me as she went through the security gate at the airport were "I want you to speak English."

(*in Cantonese*) [To do well in this country you must learn to speak English well].

(*in English*) My mother wanted all the advantages that were available to Canadian-born students to be available to me. To please her, I decided I would only speak English in school. And speaking English all day did open some doors. I had enough confidence to go on Mr. Wilson's camping trip even though I had never gone camping before and didn't know anyone else who had signed up for the trip. On that trip I met people who were born here and one or two became important friends for a while. But choosing to only speak English also closed some doors. I didn't make any friends with people from Hong Kong.

(*in Cantonese*) [I guess they thought I wasn't interested in being friends with them because I always spoke English].

(*in English*) Maybe they thought I was *juk-sin*, a banana, white-washed. I miss speaking Cantonese.

(*in Cantonese*) [I would like to be friends with others from Hong Kong. There are many things we share].

(*in English*) My mother does not know the discomfort of trying to speak English all day, every day. She is in Hong Kong where she can speak Cantonese. Some days my mouth, my cheeks, my lips, my throat hurt.

When my mother tells me, "I want you to speak English" she thinks only of the doors that might open. Not the doors that close. An English-only policy will close doors for those of us who speak other languages. Unable to say what we would like to say in English, some of us will remain silent. An English-only policy also closes doors for those of us who want to practice speaking other languages with students who already know them well. In the last few weeks, I have learned that the doors we have opened are sometimes slammed shut by an unexpected force. It is prudent to keep as many doors open as possible. Thank you.

from

Alien Creature
Linda Griffiths

Alien Creature takes place one night, when the poet, Gwendolyn MacEwen, returns to face the modern world. On this night, MacEwen is torn apart by her magic, made invincible by her magic. Revealed as drunk, lover, poet and magician, she rises to inspire and incite.

In the play, she blows bubbles immediately before this speech, this is not absolutely necessary.

GWEN

If I were to say to you, I've had many lovers, I think I'd be giving you the wrong impression. Not that I haven't had many lovers, not that I've ever counted. But to say, I have had many lovers is to present myself as a bit slutty maybe and it wasn't like that. I've been married more than a lot of people. Twice indeed. The first I won't talk about, there are too many rumours. The second I wore the veil. I took the vows. And I'm still very connected to him. The one where I wore the veil. But in between and around what I'm trying to say is that I lived in a world that was voluptuous. Where the meaning of sexual contact seems different from now. I loved all of my lovers. Loved them. Loved them. And they loved me. And when we made love, we were learning. It was the kind of thing where you could say, "sex is my sacrament" and no one would snicker. I'm not saying that living like this doesn't have any problems. I'm not saying there aren't children left over from that time knocking on doors, asking, "are you my mother?" But I do believe that some things go hand in hand and when the language of this lovemaking left, something else left too.

I wonder if I was a good lover. I'd like to think so. I'd like to think I gave something, that there was a weight to it. So I can say I've had many lovers just like I can say that I've had a lot of cocks inside me and I have. Now there are times when I think I can't stand to have one more cock in me.

Not one more. No. Go away. And so to say I've had many lovers is also to say I have paid a price. Then there are days when I sit back and smile. And I think of all the men and all they gave to me. And not just entry in the night, but the play of it. And because I knew how to play, I think maybe I was a good lover. And if things got a little tortured, things got a little tortured. We're not supposed to love drama, we're supposed to love reality. I never understood that.

I was thinking about the heart. My heart. How it pains and twitches sometimes. My heart is in a cage and my ribs are that cage and the bones are torqued and twisted. The idea that you're supposed to give your heart. Such a simple thought. And I lay beside him that night and thought, "my God I've got to do it again."

I was thinking about the words, I love you. How often with my little loves, with my many loves I've exchanged those words. To say they're tarnished would be an understatement. And I've thought they could never be said again, not by me to anyone, not by anyone to me. And then I see you. Yes, you. Don't be shy. Mr. Sensible. No, you don't have to say anything, I actually prefer my men not to speak English. Your eyes are so clear, not poisoned at all, you must drink a lot of water. I'm looking for someone to keep my Lord Death from the door. Is it you? Let's break plates like the Greeks, and dance on the shards, never cutting our feet. Let's make love in the park and shoot arrows at the moon. Let's stay up all night and…. Oh, I know. Do I want a woman like that? Men like peace, I understand. I can't offer you that. But I can offer you nights of wonder.

I reach into my mouth, down my throat, around my lungs, push aside my breastbone and pull it out.

> *GWENDOLYN reaches inside herself, as if to pull out her living heart.*

And in those minutes, hours, weeks, before I know if you will replace it with your own, I stand in the world, heartless.

from

Lament of La Sainte Catherine
Gabrielle Kemeny

We meet Catherine during the Montreal ice storm. The ice storm is in fact her masterpiece. She has transformed herself from a prostitute into a self-proclaimed guardian angel of the local diner. After uniting a host of oddballs in the diner to be "saved," Catherine settles in to watch the ensuing chaos. Catherine is a scraggly but fluently bilingual prostitute. She once got drunk and renamed herself after her favourite street corner because she didn't think "Josiane" suited her. The name stuck.

CATHERINE

    Chu née à Montréal moé, chu née à Montréal. I seen all the *merde* in this place.

Calice, do I know this town. Not like the *touristes*. With their Kodak Instaflash.

They go to see the *Stade Olympique*… then pour *la bière* Belle Gueule down their loud, sticky throats. They think they don't see me. Here. On my corner. They see Old Montreal… Notre Dame… Céline Dion. Only the lonely, quiet one, he… he comes to me.

He says: "English? French?" In "fuck" there is no language! And he will squeeze me so tight. Then go. *"Fou le camp, salot!"* I know. I know these people. I stand here and wear my skin. And wear MY *politique*. And I didn't learn it in a book. And I didn't learn it in the school. I am *le "testament sacré"*! I could be your little Mitsou *non*? *Aie.* Take it easy. I only say "I know what I know from my… ears." I hear them… whispering: the *Canadiens* fan, the hairy biker man… oooh, the Armani suit. They all come by here.

Here. *(grabs her crotch).* My narrow homeland… ahhh *que c'est tout petit, ah qu'ca coute chère.*

Vive le Quebec einh! Vive le Quebec….. libre! (exposes a shoulder) Sacrement.

"Make your choice of enemies…" mmm, so you can be really free. Well, it says that on the wall on Saint Laurent! And in the tunnel at Saint Henri: "Too many causes without a rebel." Big pink letters… as high as my thigh. So we complain. We are losing our language. Instead of *MacDonald* we say: MacDonald. Instead of *poutine*, we say poutine. Instead of slut, we say…… oh, I know. It's all… in my mouth.

(She reacts to a passerby.) Yeah? So go! Fight the danger of… *quoi? Calice.* With your big plastic glowing swords. Revenge of the bubblegum heroes and the squeaky pink bullets.

Shiny. Made in Taiwan. And the saint of the invisible ghetto? You wait for him, boys and girls. He will ride up on a *fleur-de-lis* horse and wipe you out of your "*misère.*"

Jésus de Montréal! We wait for him, *non?* Make your choice of enemies. *Maudites Anglais* French Frogs. So you like it when I talk like that? *C'est ben sale c'tte affaire, c'est ben fucké!*

I show my leg for you… because I'm proud. And because it's shit if your Grandpapa's great Grandmaman drank a cup of tea or ate croissants… back across the ocean. *C'est de la merde toute ca.* Now you are cold and selling your skin on the street, like me.

In French, in English. Same skin. Same shit. *Vive le Quebec?* Yeah. Eat your politics off my street, *bande de fuckés.* These are my people. The ones that own the street.

Oooh, and out of the dumpster at Sainte Catherine and Saint Laurent… jumps:

JÉSUS DE MONTRÉAL! He comes to me. He says… "*Calice*, you got a nice ass."

"I think I gonna save you. Even if your English, it's not so good. I am the guardian of this *sacré* place… so stop… *arrète.* For me," he says: "ass it's ass, and words it's words… and that is that."

Sacrement. He's a good type, this *Jésus de Montréal.* I hope he comes by here soon.

Do I have a present… for him.

from

The Occupation of Heather Rose
Wendy Lill

Heather Rose goes north to work on an Indian reserve. Her adventure turns into a painful exploration of her own fragile cultural heart of darkness.

HEATHER

Culture.

At orientation, we spent a whole afternoon on culture. Miss Jackson told us that going from white to Indian culture was like going from your rumpus room into your fruit cellar.

She said that cultures were all about imagining. For example, she told us when Indians looked out on a lake, they imagined shaking tents and spirit visions and powwows and canoes filled with braves moving silently across the water, thunderbirds circling overhead...

Whereas when we look out on a lake, we see something different. When I looked out on Snake Lake, I imagined hundreds of bodies lying elbow to elbow on little sandy towels, sailboats and air mattresses bobbing, tiny voices emerging from sandy radios...

Culture.

Norma Redbird lived with her new baby, her parents, her brother, her wrinkled grandmother, and five assorted others in a white frame shack no bigger than my kitchen nook and living room combined.

Part of my culture was to feel uncomfortable about barging into other people's homes uninvited, but that was my job, so I swallowed hard and...

(cheery) "Hi Norma! How's the new mom! I'm here to check you and the baby! What are you doing inside on a beautiful day like this? This is Indian

summer. *(laughs)* I've heard about your winters that last from October to May. You and little Dolores should be outside getting some fresh air, some exercise while you still can!"

Watching "Let's Make A Deal" reruns is what they were doing, all of them, including the five-day-old infant.

HEATHER looks uncomfortable, smiles, shifts about.

"The baby looks good. Good colour. Alert. Curious. That's a cute top she's wearing. I think she could use some eyedrops. Why don't you bring her in this week and I'll give her a thorough checkup."

A huge piece of frozen meat thawing out in front of the TV; Monty Hall making jokes with two women from South Dakota dressed up as chickens; me in my nurse's uniform yakking away about cute tops and eyedrops.

How did I feel? Like a spaceship which had landed in the middle of their living room, sending out little beeps.

"Spaceship Rose to earth… I've located the Indians…. What am I supposed to do now?"

Focus on food. Highlight hygiene. Win them over. Make connections.

"Oh-h-h-h… it's so *dark* in here. I saw some calico at the store for two-fifty a yard…. It would make nice curtains for those windows, and if you had some leftovers, you could make a tablecloth to cover up that oilcloth. Really brighten up the place. *(smiles nervously, fidgets)*

HEATHER pulls out some file cards from her brown bag.

"What are you having for dinner tonight? Oh… I'm not inviting myself. I just saw that piece of meat thawing on the floor. I've never *seen* such a large roast. It looks so *fresh!* Wild! But I'm trying to cut down on meat. Have you ever heard of cholesterol? It's very bad for us. Very. These are some suggestions to help us all be a little less meat-dependent. I'll just leave them here to help you with your meal planning."

HEATHER shudders, rips up her meal plans, tacks up the pieces on the bulletin board.

That day, at Norma Redbird's, was the first time I really began wondering about… a lot of things.

Someone was lying and I wasn't sure who.

Miss Jackson told us that part of Indian culture was close family ties, and that was why they lived in such cramped quarters. Bullshit. They were poor. They had no jobs. And nothing to do all day but watch reruns. And nothing to do tomorrow either. No prospects. I had never seen or tasted or smelled poverty before, and it scared me.

What did she know about Indians or family ties, or poverty or culture? All that shit about rumpus rooms and fruit cellars. And imagining. What were the Redbirds imagining—me standing there with my *Canada Food Guide* and sunburned nose, trying to out-shout two women dressed in chicken suits, telling them their house was dirty and their food disgusting. Who the hell did I think I was?

Saying someone has a different culture is just a polite way of saying they're *weird*. Not special, not privileged. Not exotic. Not mysterious at all. They're inferior. And therefore need to be helped. Translation: Altered. So much for culture! *(rips up Canada Food Guides)*

from

Divinity Bash/nine lives
Bryden MacDonald

Myrna sits in front of the curtain
on her high swivel stool.
She is wearing a terry cloth robe
that has been cut just above the knee.
Myrna has dressed the robe up a bit:
a leopard skin collar
bugle beads
and a fringe hemline.
Myrna is rambling
presumably speaking
to whoever is in the changing room
behind the wall of clothes.

MYRNA

It was the strangest clearest dream:
I was an octopus–
a big red octopus.
I loved havin all them arms–
what a feelin.
And the way you float.
You can't fall.
You can't fall underwater.
I was eating a shark—a baby shark.
Ya stun it first–
but it's still alive when you're swallowin:
that's the weird part.

But I loved that I was red
and the way that I was just sort of—suspended.
I imagine that's what an astronaut must feel like
but not with as much control:
I was in complete control.
And I'm never in control.
Well I never feel like I'm in control.
But I'm tryin to work on that.
Anyways
right in the middle of the dream
I'm in another dream:
I'm Sharon Stone in "Casino"–
rollin them dice in that great outfit.
And I win.
I win everything.
Funny eh. Dreams.
Makes ya wonder.
I mean
maybe I'm asleep right now.
Maybe I really am Sharon Stone
dreamin she has a little consignment shop.
Whatever:
I just love havin my own little place–
I just love the ambulance here.
It never occurs to ya eh?
Like I been buyin all these things for years
but all along I was buying them for someone else.
Ya see I don't look good in much
other than terry cloth bathrobes eh:
but I've made them work I think–
sort of like my own "line"—ya know?
And God knows there's lots of interesting people to talk to.
And I find just havin the little mattress in the back–
just a little place to lay my head: perfect.
And I could always put up someone in need too right?
I don't need much.
Especially after thinking I needed love.
Well–
I don't mean I don't need love.

I just don't need it that way:
the way it was.

And it's by no means all Snake's fault.
I mean
it takes two to tango
not that I know how to tango
but it does take two to do it
and we weren't—well–
we just weren't doin it good.
We weren't doin it honest.

Anyways
I had all these spare clothes around
for events I must have been imagining–
especially the maternity clothes.
Snake never wanted kids
but I guess I thought if I just kept buyin the clothes–
well anyways–
it never happened.
And probably for the best.
But me bein so scrawny all my life–
I always wanted to be big as a house
ya don't hear that often.
But it never happened.
No big deal.
And now I got the shop.
So I guess things just unfold
the way they're gonna unfold and
well
ya go with the flow I guess.
Cuz resistin it sure makes you old.
I was getting so old so fast.
Not that I don't love Snake.
Actually I think I love him more now
than I did when we were together.
But ya know
the atom just split–
whatever the fuck that means.

Anyways
I just love sayin
"Welcome to Myrna's Things Size Four to Forty."
And it's all mine.
I just gotta deal with Mom back home now–
she thinks she got three grandchildren.

from

The Exstasy of Bedridden Riding Hood
Bryden MacDonald

This is the opening monologue
from *The Exstasy of Bedridden Riding Hood*
a fantasy for three women.
Liz is a tough young delinquent
forced to do community service at a senior citizens' home after being
charged with yet another break
and enter.
She meets Gleena here
a wild old caustic broad
who believes she is the original Little Red Riding Hood.
A battle of wills ensues.
Eventually
Gleena conjures her dead grandma.
The skeptical Liz is enlightened.
All three live happily ever after.

Like those dreams
when you know you're awake:
A mutable world of shadow and light.

The plaintive howl of a
lone wolf.

LIZ listens.

She is a young tough
worn and ready to rumble
Blue jeans
T-shirt
no bra

leather jacket
serious boots.

LIZ wanders the shadows
Thinking out loud
Creating a world
she is both remembering and experiencing.

LIZ
Once upon a time
not too long ago
and not so far away
in a land of bullshit and confusion
there was a little girl
who had the strangest clearest dreams.
In these dreams
she was always awake
but still lost in a deep deep sleep.

Once
she woke up gasping
and bolted out of bed.
She smelled smoke.
The clock radio was dead.
The lamp wouldn't turn on.
The toaster oven was off.
The ashtrays were all damp.
She smelled smoke.

She lights a candle and wanders into a grey flannel hallway.
She stumbles toward an exit light
and down seventeen flights of stairs.
She is in an empty lobby.
She runs outside and into the city.
She still smells smoke.

She looks up at the building–
it is unfamiliar:
lights flicker in every window
like a huge wall of snow filled TVs.

She starts to walk.
She walks and walks.
Her footsteps click.
She still smells smoke.

The street lamps
look like tall arched silver birch
and she can't see below her knees
because of the steam rising from the manhole covers.

Or is it fog?

Or is it smoke?

Neon bleeds through the soupy atmosphere
and she feels like she is going to blow up
but she is whistling.
She could never whistle before.
She keeps walking
deeper into the murky night.
She still smells smoke
but now
it tastes like vanilla or eucalyptus.
Her eyes begin to water
and she feels like she is made out of tin:
her heart clatters in her chest.

By now
candle drippings have covered her clenched hands
and she notices she is naked.
Suddenly–
she is thinking of her childhood.

It is very present.
She grinds her teeth.
She is remembering crying over a snared rabbit
when she was seven years old.
It's bleating is unbearable.
Her father is comforting her.
The other hunters are laughing.
She runs deeper into the woods.

Then just as suddenly
she is alone again
and there are two moons in the sky
which is now forest green
with a wet iridescent glow
scalloped and layered like fish scales.

The moons are slit through the centre.
They blink.
They are eyes.
The sky shimmers
and unfolds into wings.
She is looking at a dragon.
The smoky smell pumps from two large nostrils.

The little girl becomes shy
and lowers her head.
The caked wax on her hands turns to fur.
Her back arches.
She can see her own nose.
She howls.
She is a wolf.
And apparently the dragon is her friend.

Her thoughts become luminous.
Her history is clear:
she is an outcast from a pack of
pirate wolves.
Her front left paw
is caught in the jaws of a rusty trap.

The dragon's chest is pierced with a silver spear.
A tear from the dragon's eye drenches her
and the trap on her paw dissolves.

With a burst of strength
she leaps onto the chest of the dragon
and pulls the spear from her with her strong new teeth.
The smoke is gone.
She is in a garden.
She breathes clear.

The dragon is gone
and instead there is a woman
with fiery hair that crackles and sparks
and pale green eyes with black diamond irises.
She blows a kiss and is gone.

The little girl stands alone
in a stand of silver birch.
Trumpeter swans crease the sky.
Tiny soldiers straddle their necks
grasping reigns of vines.
A huge turtle flies by next.
There is laughter in the air.
Her path is clear.
She does not need bread crumbs.

> *LIZ lights a cigarette*
> *with a Zippo lighter.*

I wake up in my lumpy cot
in my shitty dank room
with that sinking feeling.
And once again I wonder
if maybe I should seek professional help.
Why haven't I been recalled?
They recall cars when they're fucked up–
why not people?

I lay there for awhile in the usual way–
like I'm embedded in concrete.
Booze bottles
like dead soldiers
everywhere.
I count the sunglasses scattered around the room.
I have twenty-seven pairs
but no clean socks.
Why didn't my parents force me to wash dishes when I was a child?
Because they were never there.

Sadly
I have an answer for everything
and am convinced
that my parents had me
just to prove to the world that they were having sex.

I drag my sad ass
to the filthy bathroom I share
with the other derelicts
in this sad excuse for a boarding house.
I run the water till the rust is gone
splash my face
and head off for my first day of "Community Service."
one B&E too many.
"Some people collect stamps
I collect sound systems–
you got a problem with that?"
That's what I said to Officer Power
when he came sniffing around my door.
And yes—that was his real name.
Anyway
firm warning equals "Community Service":
The Braewood Seniors' Hideaway.
Calling bingo
and reading *Jonathan Livingston Seagull*
to smelly old has-beens
dumped by their own children for their own good.

Oh well–
better than a poke in the eye with a sharp stick.

"Agnete"
from

The Danish Play
Sonja Mills

Summer 1940, Denmark has just been invaded by the Nazis. Eager not
to be seen as tyrants, the Nazis allow nightclubs and theatres to remain
open (for now). Agnete Ottosen, who will later resist the occupation with
devastating results, has a friend Michael who runs an open mic night at
a small playhouse. He has asked her many times to come and read her
poetry to the friendly and often drunk crowd; tonight she does.

AGNETE

     I opened the daily newspaper to page three, to see if the Mrs.
and Miss column might have a smart idea. The questions women ask!
Can a woman work in an office when she has become a mother-in-law
considering her son-in-law works in the same office on minimum wage?
Can she walk in Bishop's Square with shoes that are too small and silk
stockings when there's a good foot of water? Answer, reader: there's not
a thing a woman can't do. She can exchange a sparrow for a duck. And she
can walk to her grave as the Madonna though she has twins. And she can
tell a man that she prefers love over money.

But can a woman dance the Charleston while she's breastfeeding? Would
she risk that the milk became butter? Can she relax at Marie Christensen's
all day long and eat fatty cakes when she wants to be skinny as a rail?
Should she ask for tea when it's really coffee she wants? Can she go sledding
wearing a skirt, or should she wear trousers? (Why not ask: Can she go
skiing at the Eagle's Nest?) And can she go to a costume party the same day
she's doing laundry? And can she pretend to be Venus when she's 110 kilos?
And is she dumb and unsure because she's forgotten her age? And can she
make applesauce if her pears are a little soft? Answer, reader: there's not
a thing a woman can't do.

It's said that one lunatic can ask more than ten of the country's wisest trolls
can answer, and I can see that old truth still applies in the "Mrs. and Miss"

column in the daily newspaper. Can a woman walk home alone when she lives at the Magdalena home? And can she hold her head high if she prefers to nurse her own children? And will she have the same luck in love as her mother who was divorced as late as last year? Answer, reader: in all the hours of the day and night she can swing her hips and even if she has turned 100 and still prefers to have a boy's haircut and she wears dresses that barely reach the knee though her ankles are as big as an elephant's thigh, there's isn't a thing a woman can't do.

from

Annie Mae's Movement
Yvette Nolan

Anna Mae is isolated onstage in a pool of light. She is wearing jeans, and a "ghost shirt." On her wrist is a large turquoise bracelet. She is doing karate moves.

ANNA

There are all kinds of ways of getting rid of people. In Central America they disappeared people. Just came and took them away in the middle of the night, whoosh gone, and then deny everything. Very effective. Well, here they disappear people too. They disappear them by keeping them underfed, keeping them poor, prone to sickness and disease. They disappear them into jails. In jails they disappear their dignity, their pride. They disappear our kids, scoop 'em up, adopt 'em out, they never see their families again.

Our leaders—the leaders of the American Indian Movement—said that we should learn to fight. And because we'd never get enough firearms, we had to use the only thing that they couldn't take away from us. We had to train our bodies, turn our hands into weapons. All right, I said, right on, and I got up at dawn to train with the rest of them. Well, they didn't mean me, did they? They didn't mean the women. They meant the men, the warriors, the dog soldiers. Not you, girl, fighting's not for you. But my first husband, Jake, he ran a martial arts school…

I guess I got it from my mother, she used to fight with the Indian Agent. This one time, he brought us bunch of clothes, *donations*—army coats and what do you call those pants they wear riding horses?—all moth-eaten, full of holes. I couldn't have been more than four, but I remember she sent him packing, with his crummy rags. After that, he finally started sending us better stuff. After *that*, she'd write letters to Halifax, to Ottawa, every time he pissed her off.

You gotta stand up, you gotta fight for what's important, no matter who wants to shut you up. We have to fight, even if it seems like we're fighting ourselves. Or else we will disappear, just disappear.

At that AIM meeting in Wisconsin, when Myrtle waited all morning for her turn at the mike, waited through all the leaders, all the big boys recounting all the victories for Indian people, when she finally got to the mike, they called for lunch, for LUNCH. And she stood there and she started to talk anyway, and our leaders took the mike away from her, covered it up with their hands so she couldn't be heard, all she wanted was to ask where are our children? How many of us have lost our children, or know someone who has lost children this way? They wouldn't even let her speak. No business here, they said.

Our children disappeared and our women silenced.

It's so easy to disappear people in this country, especially Indian people. Scoop 'em up here, drop 'em off there. Whoosh, gone. They just deny everything.

Anna Mae? Anna Mae Who? Never heard of her...

Whoosh...

> *She is gone.*

from

Not the End
Shelley Sereda

Tawni is following her dream and only hope that represents a chance at a new beginning from her otherwise shaky world. She recently escaped from the world of prostitution, to start a new life as an actor, which she thought might lead to a better life. As she is performing in her first show ever, which the audience shares with her over the duration of the play, she breaks all the rules of the theatre, such as speaking directly to the audience, breaking in and out of character, and expressing herself without inhibition. As the play progresses, Tawni sheds her fears and inhibitions to eventually reveal her true self.

TAWNI

I don't know what else I would do. It's not that I can't do anything else. It's just that… after trying it, I don't want to do anything else. And I can't go back to hooking. But it's hard not to. I mean, if this doesn't work out… what other options do I have?

My roomie, Kate, you'll probably meet her later… she's still doing it. Hooking. And I'm scared for her. I still don't know what happened to me to make me change my mind about all this. I'm just trying to get my shit back together… my life. Because I was sinking fast. I would've hit rock bottom pavement soon. And I'm tougher than Kate. I can take more shit and still walk away standing. But why? Why put up with all the bullshit?

I never used to see things this way, until I stepped back from everything, and saw Kate. My best friend. The stuff she talks about… the other girls and their latest gossip, how tripped out they got last night, how some fucking asshole got out of hand and beat the living shit out of some girl. "Oh, it's okay" she says. "You don't even know her… she's new." It's fucking scary. What's scarier… is that Kate talks about this shit like it's okay… like it's just another day. And for her, it is just a typical day. It kills me to know that my best friend is actually doing this to herself. It's no life… not for anyone. It's fucking suicide. Slow and painful.

But when you're caught up in it, you can justify the shit out of why you do it. Well, why not? If the demand's there, somebody's gotta fill it, right? And it's good fucking money, so why shouldn't I?

Problem is… I've only met a few… a few rare girls, who can put up with hooking themselves, without doing some sorta shit to tolerate it. Everyone's got their drug… smokes, alcohol, coke, crack, E… whatever gets you through the day. Funny thing is… near the end… I couldn't even really remember many of those days. If any. It's all a fucking blur.

I'd stay up doing coke, until every couple of days, I'd either pass out, or just finally get some sleep. Trying to get some sleep meant lying in bed, tripping out, because I couldn't get my mind to stop thinking "If only I had just one more line." I'd toss and turn, not being able to shut my eyes for at least the first two hours. And eventually, I'd come down and sleep. Though, I can't really remember falling asleep. But I remember that my arm… sometimes… it would go limp… like it was dead… a dead weight. It's like your leg when it falls asleep… but worse. It was hard to wake up my arm… like waking it from a coma. And it still happens, if I fall asleep on my arm. It's like I must have killed it. I guess the drugs killed it. I don't know what the fuck's wrong with it. But it's not like I can go to the doctor and tell him what happened. First of all, I don't know what really happened to it because I was so fucked up on coke, and, secondly, I ain't exactly going to tell a doctor why I don't remember what happened. That I used to be a coke head.

from

Vita

Ivana Shein

The play takes place on three trains, during three different decades and three different wars. Sarah 2's character lives in the present, during the "War on Evil" and throughout the play is piecing together the stories of her grandmother, her mother and her younger self.

After Sarah 2's birth mother dies, she travels through Austria by train for a modelling job, and is haunted by her grandmother, Vita. She spends the entire play resisting her grandmother's story and her own past until this moment in the play when she admits to her grandmother how much she needs to know, and live, the truth of who she is.

SARAH 2

When Josephine died, my mother, (that still sounds weird to me), when she died everything changed. I was frantic. Obsessed. Running around trying to make myself perfect. For ten years I tried to make myself a different person. I got a nose job, liposuction, I got my eyes done. Everything on me went under the knife. And I became a model. But really I just went further back. I went so far back and so far inside that I couldn't tell what was real or what was just my imagination. Hunger does that to you too. I could smell where I came from, but I never spoke of it. It was always to be quiet the fact that I was Jewish, it was a secret. Or a joke depending on the day. We lived around this precious lie. My adopted parents, or my fake parents as I liked to call them, got Easter eggs and Christmas trees and silent. No one was to ever speak. There would be no words. There was only to be this clean prettiness. A crisp silence. Like white linen. But somehow the silence wasn't large enough to cover the truth. And the darkness, and the reality slipped out from under me at the oddest times. I'm sick of that. I want to speak. I want to speak to you my grandmother. I want you to be known. I want to know you. And stay up late listening to your stories. I want to be your stories, I want to let these suitcases go. I want to open them and watch the past fly outside. My fake parents were Jewish too. They hid it also. I remember walking into the living room one day and my fake father was writing a letter. I asked him who he was writing it to, and, he said, I should never sneak up on people like that. I found out later that for twenty-five years every Sunday he would write a letter to his parents in Russia, and he never once mentioned that he had married a Christian woman and had become a Protestant minister. He told me once, that he wanted to fight anti-Semitism from within the Church. But I wonder if he was fighting it in the Church, or in himself. He turned and looked at me with such a look of shame, that day. Like I had walked in on him doing something so wrong. My fake mother told me we must never speak of such things. That it just wouldn't be nice. And as we know nice is the goal. That's when I left them and went looking for you. Went to find you. To tell you that you may be dead, but you are not alone. That I am here. Not forgetting you. Ever.

"My Goalie"
from

The Games We Play
Danielle Skene

Monique, a huge hockey fan, explains her obsessive relationship with her number one player.

MONIQUE

I LOVE YOU! *(She waits for a response but none comes.)* I know he can hear me. That's why I never yell it during the game. I understand his need for total concentration. It is not like I'm a groupie, and I am not just a fan, I'm a believer. I remember the first time I saw him. He looked like a god, ready for combat as he glided out onto the ice. It was like his body was framed in an otherworldly mist. I realise now that's because my face was pressed up against the glass—but that is exactly why I know it's true love because normally, I don't like to attract attention to myself, but here I am, screaming my undying devotion for someone who wouldn't acknowledge me if he bumped into me in the parking lot…. Well, maybe he would. I like to think he would. An autograph would be nice, maybe a T-shirt, a game jersey is a bit too much to ask—but if by chance he had it on him, I wouldn't say no. After all, I am here every home game.

I have my routine for good luck. It is exactly the same every time, every move, every gesture, every action, exactly the same. Arrive at 6:05 on the dot, park in Section C, have my ticket ripped by Martin, who is always at turnstile #3, order a giant pretzel from the kiosk on the second level but then decide not to take it and get a beer instead. Take the stairs up to my section, see the enormity of the arena, take a big surprised breath in *(does so)* and drop my beer. I have to be pretty wily on this last bit because the maintenance crew is starting to get very suspicious. Once all that's done, sit in seat 45 of Section 201. All of this must be accomplished by 6:40 so I can be sitting down and ready for his warm-up ritual. This is when I first fell in love. It was the most beautiful thing I had ever seen. Oh, he starts out like everyone else. Skate, skate, shuffle, shuffle, skate, skate but then, he moves to his net, stares at it for a good minute, not moving a muscle and then, he starts to dance. You can't call it anything else. It seems very obvious to me what he is doing but I think that is because I have an instinct for these things. Male fans are very uncomfortable with this idea because to them, dancing on ice is called figure skating and that's faggy. But I don't care what anyone else says—he dances. He shimmies his shoulders, grinds his hips, slides from side to side and in a move that would make a Solid Gold dancer rip off his lamé with envy, he drops to the ice in a full Russian splits. The first time I saw it I thought I was going to wet myself. He is the most beautiful thing I have ever seen. It is the same every time. I feel it is our special little moment. No one else ever seems to notice what is going on. He might not show it, and he would never admit it, but he is dancing just for me. And he knows I'm watching. That's love.

"Anne"
from

Shakespeare's Will
Vern Thiessen

Anne Hathaway reads the will that her husband, William Shakespeare, has left after his death, freely expressing how each item on the list makes her feel. She recounts the loss of their son, Harry, and how she feels Shakespeare punishes her for this in his will.

ANNE

"In the name of God, Amen.
I, William Shakespeare
of Stratford-upon-Avon
in the county of Warwick
gentlemen
in perfect health and memory…"

Yes yes yes…

"Item:
I give and bequeath unto my daughter Judith
one hundred and fifty pounds of lawful English money…
…in discharge of her marriage portion…"

Ahh. Bribing her to marry, I see.

> *She flips forward a page.*

"Item:
I give, will, bequeath, and devise
unto my eldest daughter Susanna…
to have and to hold
all during the term of her natural life,

all my goods, chattel, leases, plate, jewels,
and household stuff whatsoever
And after her decease
to the first song of her body lawfully issuing, and to the heirs…

…male…

…of her body…"

Pause.

I see. Lineage.

She finds another spot.

"Item:
To Hamnet Sadler 26 shillings and eight pence to buy him a ring…
And to my fellows in the theatre
John Hemings, Richard Burbage, and Henry Condell
26 shillings and 8 pence a piece
to buy them all rings…"

She rubs her ring finger.

Rings… (*wry*) Even though… even though…!

She reads more.

"Item:
I give and bequeath
unto my sister Joan
20 pounds
and all my wearing apparel
and I do will and devise unto her…

…the house in Stratford…

wherein she may dwelleth
for her natural life…"

She re-reads this to herself, confused.

The house…
The house…?
But…

    Pause.

"Item: I give unto my wife Anne…"

    She turns over the leaf, reads to self, then:

"I give unto my wife Anne…
…my second best bed…"

    Pause.

"…with the furniture…"

    She flips the pages, but there is no more. Pause.

And so this is…
this is my, my…
for, for…

"He never forgot you know…
He never…"

(*steady*) It happened so silently
me reading
Susanna making sandcastles
Judith and Harry
playing together in shallow surf.

Judith runs in
teeth clacking like a skeleton
and I pull a blanket around her.

I look up
Harry is now twenty feet out
waving
laughing.
He mouths something
but the gull's cry
drowns him out.

I wave back
shoo away a wasp
and look up again
to see him gone.

And I,
I think
but where, where,
and I look up and down the shore
but still he is, he is, and I just saw him, where?
and I run to the water's edge, call to him, and the girls
they splash in, and I say no, there are currents and I, I
look for Brundage to help but he, high above, on the cliff,
and I call for help, but he cannot hear me, and I turn back,
and I—

     She gulps air and plunges forward.

—rush into the sea, my gowns heavy with water, and
Susanna yells:
No!
You will sink Mother
you will sink
and I tear if off:
my blouse, my shoes, my gown, my…

     She tears away some of her clothing.

trying to
to become a fish
to swim to you

Harry!!
Harry!!

    She catches her breath.

And he
waving goodbye
like you
at the road's end
pack slung over you shoulder
waving
waving…

    Pause.

For hours
I hoped
the ocean would take pity
throw him up
spout him out
like Jonah
alive.

    Pause.

And
to have Brundage
deliver him to me
pulled from a grave so wet.
And to hold him in my arms
to pull away the cold kelp
wrapped around his neck like a noose.

    Pause.

And
not to bring him home
but instead to burn him on the beach that night
for his body, bloated had…

And
to carry his ashes
in a box cut from birch
to hold him on my lap one last time
three days back in the carriage
and to lower it in the ground
and to hear the church bell toll
like a ship
so far away, so far…

She grabs the will, her anger mounting.

And with *this*
you blame me?
with *this* you punish me?
with these *words*
you break it
our promise
with this
you rip in two
our vow
with this
you
you…

In a rage she wants to rip his papers into pieces. She starts to do so, grabbing the sheaves, but cries out.

No, no, no, no, no! I will not suffer this, I will not!

She tosses the will aside.

A long, long pause, as she takes the time to compose herself.

Then she hears something.

A bell, but it seems far away. She listens.

I will go back.

> *Pause.*

Yes.

> *Pause.*

I will go back.

I will go back to the sea
to live like my father.
I will go back to the sea
to be near my only son.
I will go back to the sea
to turn back time
to let the waves
wash my wounds clean
of consequence
of memory
of *words*.

> *She finds his poem. She reads:*

"Those lips that Love's own hand did make
Breath'd forth the sound that said I hate...
'I hate' from hate away she threw,
And sav'd my life, saying 'not you'..."

"Karen"
from

The Begats
Paula Wing

The opening speech from *The Begats*, a raucous comedy about the tragedy of not being able to choose your family. Karen Ambrose is Canada's foremost expert on swallowing, though she can't get any respect at home. Facing a crisis in both her personal and professional lives she's called home to deal with a crisis. Or so she thinks.

KAREN

It's an intimate act at the heart of life. We do it all the time and it never even occurs to us that our life depends on it. It's critical to our survival and it's not breathing. *(She points out someone in the audience.)* You just did it. *(points out another person)* So did you. You too.

I speak, of course, about the act of swallowing. If the one hundred muscles involved did not act in co-ordination, food would simply fall down the windpipe, fill up our lungs, and choke us to death. Have I got your attention?

Swallowing can be divided into two halves: one voluntary and the other involuntary. The first half, the voluntary part, is very familiar. Once food has been well chewed and mixed with saliva, the tongue takes it to the back of the mouth and voluntary muscles push it here, into the pharynx. It is the sensation, the actual *feeling* of food hitting the back of the throat that triggers the second—involuntary—half.

Now comes a series of movements that are rapid, powerful, and difficult to stop. The food enters the pharynx causing the epiglottis, which is actually a flap of cartilage, to close over the larynx, or voice box, here. This cuts off the path to the lungs, here. That one small movement rescues each of us from suffocation hundreds of times a day.

Yes I get passionate. Some people even think I exaggerate because this life-saving epiglottis is my particular area of interest and expertise. Believe me, I don't need to exaggerate! When you watch it in action over several years as I have, when you experience its strength, flexibility and split-second timing, you'll be as excited as I am. But let's not get stuck on the epiglottis just yet. We have to finish our textbook swallow first.

We pick up the action in the midst of the epiglottal movement, which causes the sphincter at the top of the esophagus to relax. A sphincter, by the way, is simply a circular muscle—just to avoid any—geographical confusion. Little joke there! Some people think I don't have a sense of humour but in this work it's critical. So this particular sphincter opens and the muscles of the pharynx seize the food and squeeze it into what we call a bolus, which in non-technical terms is simply a rounded lump. The bolus, or lump, is then forced into the esophagus, which propels the food toward the stomach. Finally, the muscle at the entry to the stomach relaxes and allows the bolus to pass.

Now we've refreshed ourselves with the basics. It's time to dive in and specialise.

from

Veranda

Betty Jane Wylie

Karin is a member of an Icelandic family settled in Gimli, Manitoba. She has become *Fjallkona* (Maid of the Mountain), an honour bestowed on a woman of the Icelandic Canadian Community. Part of her duty is to give a speech at *Islendingadagurinn*, Icelandic Celebration Day.

KARIN

My dear friends, today you have honoured me and my family more deeply than I can say. It is a great privilege for me to stand before you as your Maid of the Mountain for 1950 and speak to you as compatriot, neighbour, and friend.

Those of you who know me well will have trouble relating my present dignity to the agony of the little girl who slid down the old wooden slide on Gimli Public School and got a bottom full of slivers. My father carried me home and my mother picked out all the slivers while he told me stories from the sagas to keep my mind occupied, never reminding me that I had been forbidden to play on the slide.

Instead, he told me about Egil, who taunted the gods and won reprieve with his art.

I had forgotten about the sliver and about Egil until just recently when I read the sagas, in preparation for this day.

And then there was this time I went horseback riding, also against orders, on a skittish horse that ran away with me. I stayed on, but my ankles were lacerated and bloody because I had no boots.

Again my father carried me home—a good deal heavier by this time—and poured me a brandy while Mama washed away the dirt and the tears and waited for the doctor to come. My first brandy, it is a shocking thing for a Maid of the Mountain to confess that she began drinking at the tender age of eleven! It eased the pain, as I remember, and I did not become a drunkard.

Later, when I was seventeen, some friends and I were stranded by a sudden storm on the lake, My father found us the next morning, beached on the far side of Hecla Island—safe, but cold and hungry.

The other parents scolded their children, though we were not children, and questioned them fearfully as to their behaviour overnight. My father never questioned me. He trusted me, always.

My father and mother taught me to speak Icelandic as I speak it to you now, and made me learn to read it and write it, against my will, for it was extra homework I didn't want when I was a girl. I am grateful for it now.

My father and my late brother Svenn taught me to love the Icelandic sagas and to realise that we are all of us still living a saga in a new land.

My father and my mother instilled in me the reverence for our past, the will to endure against all odds, and the serenity to accept what life offers us and to go on. I have not always been serene, I admit to you, but I have ever had the example of my father and mother before me.

When I go with you to lay the wreath on the cairn, it will be with humility and gratitude for the courage, love, and wisdom of our ancestors—and of my father and mother.

she speaks

MOTHERS

"Twinkle"
Nina Aquino

Twinkle, a young Filipino, writes a letter to her mother while on a plane to Canada.

TWINKLE

Dear 'Nay… Mrs. Madlansacay told me that I should start practicing my writing in English. So I guess I should start now.

(takes a deep breath) How are you 'Nay? Me? I'm doing wonderful… excellent. I was not feeling too well a while ago but I think I am okay now… well… to be honest, I was scared at first actually… I thought the plane would never take off! It seemed to go 'round and 'round and 'round the runway forever. I said to myself, "If this plane turns around one more time, I'm getting off. That's it." But it didn't make another turn. It took off at the last minute that I decided to stay. I started panicking because I was thinking, "What am I doing here? I shouldn't be here… this is a mistake…" I grabbed my seatbelt and tried to take it off but my hands were stiff… *(starting to slowly relive the panic)* and then I couldn't breathe… and my legs were shaking and… and… *(screaming)* "Oh my God! Stop! Stop! Stop the plane! I'm not supposed to be here! Stop please!" But the clouds were all around us already. Nobody heard me… nobody even cared. Here I was… up in the air… going further and further away.

Tell me why I'm here again, 'Nay? I need to remember why I'm on this plane… because… 'Nay, I'm scared… I'm really scared and it's lonely and the plane is not going to turn around. This is for the best, right? This is for my own good, right? You said I needed to do this for my future… "good school, good job, good money… help me and your Tatay"… well, I'm here 'Nay and I don't see anything but clouds and all these people who can't even hear me yell.

What if Canada is like this? Huh? What if I yell and scream for help and nobody can hear me because I'm this small, invisible, brown, nobody looking for what? Her future? What if it's not there? Huh? 'Nay? What if it's right back home... where all my friends are... where you and Tatay are... where my heart is.

The pretty stewardess came up to me and said, "hello" and asked if I was okay and if I needed anything. "Can you make this plane turn around? Can you bring me back home?" I wanted to tell her that but of course, I didn't... 'Nay, of course not. I will be brave and fearless like you told me to be. *(almost chant-like)* I won't disappoint you. I won't disappoint you. I won't disappoint you. *(whispering to herself)* I can't disappoint you. All your sacrifices... all your hard work just to send me all the way to Canada. I'm not allowed to disappoint you, right?

> *Beat.*

Dear 'Nay... Mrs. Madlansacay told me that I should start practicing my writing in English. So I guess I should start now. How are you 'Nay? Me? I'm doing wonderful... excellent. I'm looking forward to seeing Canada. *(tries to hold back the tears)* I can't wait... my future is bright and straight ahead. Right, 'Nay? I can't wait...

At the Full and Change of the Moon
Dionne Brand

BOLA

We try to live peacefully and quietly. I make small things for our mother and I bring her paradise plums and sugar. And I shine the part of the floor that I made into an ocean for her. We live peacefully and quietly and you would not know that we are living there except sometimes for my recitations and our mother's instructions. It is a quiet house as my mother loved it, quiet and calm. The backyard is quiet and the windows are quiet and now and then the trees move and the rain falls and my mother and I sit on the back steps and watch.

Sometimes I can't sleep because I'm afraid I'll wake up and it will be like that morning when our mother went to the Paradise Cemetery, but then I fall asleep and wake up and there she is sitting on the bed in her blue dress with the lace and it is a morning with sweet light coming through the window and the guava tree is either leafy or bare and I am lying on the floor at the foot of our mother's bed and my fear leaves.

It is my birthday. Our mother told me to bathe and clean myself off and get ready for my birthday cake. I am so happy. I have cleaned myself off and here I am in the gallery, waiting for my mother to bring out my birthday cake. I can't but smile to myself at how well our mother has planned this party. I can smell the baking, the sweet flour and the vanilla essence. Every now and again our mother calls to me to make haste and put on my clothes for the party.

I am waiting for my best dress to dry. I am sitting here in the gallery, letting the sun dry my body, and when the neighbours look over I tell them that our mother is making me a party. The sun is so warm. It spreads all over the gallery and if I close my eyes for long and let it in, deep into my eyelids, when I open my eyes everything is dazzling. The street is dazzling and the trees are dazzling and my skin is dazzling. I close my eyes and smell our mother's baking and I open my arms and let the sun warm my whole body.

"Mary"
from

Grace and After
Drew Carnwath

Grace and After is a collection of urban vignettes, based on the myth of Orpheus and Eurydice, set on New Year's Eve. The play explores themes of modern spirituality; fate versus coincidence; and the search for grace in the face of its opposite—disgrace. Mary is a television actor who is summoned home by her father on New Year's Eve.

MARY

Standing at the top of the escalator. Toronto Airport:
Fluorescent lights, soft carpeting, muted voices.
Greys and browns and light blues that go on forever.
The taste of aluminum on my tongue and teeth, of jet fuel,
of hard candy cane.
Of waiting to meet my father
on the last day of the year.
The escalator takes me down.

I was in Vancouver, shooting a movie of the week
based on a true story
about a mom with a second-rate cheerleader for a daughter.
A true story about a jealous mom who hired a hitman to kill the star
cheerleader on the squad so her own daughter would have a chance.
My first Christmas away from home.

I was supposed to play a lawyer in this movie of the week
when I got a call from my father.
It was an emergency, he said.
He had to see me, he said.
It was about Mom.
The escalator takes me down.

And isn't it funny—At this very moment I can see my father now.
He's down below stepping on the "up" escalator.
He doesn't see me yet. He looks like someone else until I catch his eye.

The escalator takes me down
and he's going up
and we meet halfway
we're eye to eye we're equal just for a moment
and we make a funny face.
Then the moment passes and we pass and I remember why I'm here.

The escalator takes me down. Toronto Airport.
I breathe in the sound of Christmas whispers
of other families' reunions
of old stories made new again.
I am surrounded by the sound of newspaper headlines:

Echoes of children who say their last goodbye
on the Bloor Street Viaduct.
Whispers of children found hanging from coat racks
at their private schools.
Murmurs of a faceless nameless monster
who roams the underground looking for children
to pull in front of fast-moving subways.

The escalator takes me down. Toronto Airport.
I grip the rubber railing as I prepare to tell my father
about the times my mother left me alone at home
while she went out drinking at the Buccaneer Tavern.
I prepare to tell him the story of having to call the bar
and asking the bartender, please, if my mother is there,
could she please come home now?
I prepare to tell him the story of my mother coming home
smelling of peanuts and smoke,
and asking her about the Buccaneer Tavern,
and how she tried to make a joke of it by saying
"Friends, Romans, Countrymen: lend me your Buccaneers!"

And I prepare to tell him about the look on my mother's face,
when I didn't laugh at her jokes.

I am at the bottom of the escalator now,
looking up,
as I wait for my father.
Toronto Airport. Automatic doors open and close
cold winds sneak into the corridors from the runway.
As I reach for my father I remember night swimming.
The only time it felt okay to be afraid.
Surrounded by the cold and wet, looking up to see…. Nothing.
Underwater at night.

As I touch my father
I remember a time when my mother was alive
Which is why I'm here
Which is why I don't remember who cried first
As we hold each other up
At the bottom of the escalator
At Toronto Airport
On the last day of the year.

"Rhonda"
from

Natural Death
Sally Clark

A woman (Rhonda) is onstage. Her hair is dyed a flamboyant shade of red. She wears an expensive-looking pantsuit that was fashionable in the 1970s. It is tight-fitting.

RHONDA

It's a bit like Natural Childbirth. The principle's the same 'cept it's the opposite. They die. But it's Natural and Natural's the way things should be. Mother drank a lot and she was depressed. And yeah, maybe I should have taken her out for lunch. A lunch at The Seasons might have cheered her up. *(laughs)* I never thought of that. Anyway, it's too late now. It's amazing how long it takes for someone to die. That's the weird thing. You think, oh hey, she'll be gone in a week. But it takes forever.

At the start, Mother was looking pretty awful. She'd stopped eating and she drank gin all day. She knew she had liver cancer so she didn't want to bother the doctors. Turned out she didn't have liver cancer at all. Died of starvation, but live and learn, I say. We didn't see any point in her going to a doctor and we didn't see any point in bringing one in.

Mother had been saying she wanted to die ever since Dad died. That was like twelve years ago so we figured it was time. Yeah, she had a say in it, too. It wasn't like it was just me making all the decisions. But you know, it's really annoying. Twelve years of listening to her moan that life wasn't worth living and what the hell did it matter if she did get drunk. Twelve years of wanting to end it all. She finally gets there and she changes her mind?!

I said, "Ma, you can't change your mind now. You're gonna die." She says— "I don't want to die!" I said—"Well, I'm sorry but it's too late. You've done all the wrong things for the last twelve years. Smoked too many cigarettes. Became an alcoholic. It's just too late." Well, she didn't like that so I said—

"Look Ma, we're having a Natural Death here. It's like the Lamaze classes I took 'cept it's the opposite. You learn how to stop breathing." Then I put the pillow over her head and that was that. Just kidding. I have two delightful children. Jason and Amber. Amber's in Tibet right now learning how to be a Buddhist monk. And Jason's a street hustler. He sells real-estate part-time. And yeah, you might think, Geez, that's pretty sleazy but you know, we're upper middle-class and it really doesn't matter how many drugs we do or how many strangers we fuck, we're always going to be upper middle-class.

Ma's house helps. It'll fetch a good price. *(laughs)* Real estate's crazy in Vancouver. It's true, in a way. Ma's kept us all upper middle-class. I had this friend. He used to be upper middle-class but not anymore. He ran out of money. That's cause he lost his parents early on. Still, he thought he was invincible. Inherited all his parent's furniture and broke it. Couldn't sit in it properly. Felt bad about it but when you're a drug addict, you can only sit in certain types of chairs. The delicate antique types—well, ya break 'em.

Mother started flailing her arms about when I used the pillow so I took it away. Boy, was she mad. That's when she turned against the Natural Death idea. "Call the doctor, you bitch!" Her language got all weird, too. Mother was always a stickler for language. Hated it when I called her Ma. Said it was common. I went out with this guy years ago. He taught me how to be common and it stuck.

So, Mother's swearing up a storm and I thought, Christ I can't listen to this till it's over so I called a doctor who's a friend of mine. She took one long look at her and said, "I wish you'd called me sooner. She's dying." Now, a doctor's always going to say that. I wish you'd called me sooner. When? Twelve years ago when Dad died? Five years ago when Mother started ordering her gin by the case? If someone gets it into their head that they're gonna die, then you can't stop them.

At the actual Death. Well, that was amazing. Though it took a helluva long time cause Mother decided she wanted to live, instead. She fought. Apparently, they always fight at the end. But the Death—you know when you run a dog over with your car. By accident, of course, but you know how it is when it's run over. The body goes into a spasm and you actually see the light start to go out of their eyes. And the eyes stare at you, you know. They give you That Look. And it stays with you. Ma gave me That Look. And then she was dead.

It was fabulous! I feel reborn. I thought it was exciting when I did my Natural Births. But this is better. There's something really spiritual about Death. I feel like a new person. People think it's weird me wearing her clothes. But they were there. Big huge walk-in closet full. Vintage designer clothes. Who wouldn't wear them? I feel close to Ma when I'm in her clothes. And what's really funny is I actually like her now. Hated her guts when she was alive. But I slip this little number on and we're friends again.

Everyone today's told me I look just like her. And I don't even mind. Isn't that a kick! Dying my hair helps, sixties' bouffant style but it's come back so why not? And the outfit. Yeah, I never thought people would be wearing this stuff again but they are. *(laughs)* Everything old is new again!

"Charlotte" by Charlotte Corbeil-Coleman
from

The End of Pretending

Emily Sugerman and Charlotte Corbeil-Coleman

Charlotte, fifteen, is spending the summer with her best friend Emily in
a small town. Her mother is dying and her form of denial is to hide it
from Emily. The first half of this monologue comes at the beginning of
the play explaining why it would be easier if Emily and her were just the
stereotypes of typical best friends, one loud and one quiet, instead of
a confusion of both. The second half is the monologue that ends the play.

CHARLOTTE

If only it was that easy. If only we could be categorised into small
boxes and properly labelled. If only I could just be out there, loud and
friendly, instead of awkward, nervous, living in discomfort. Petrified of
salespeople, of ordering. If only I didn't shut off when I got to a certain
point at a party when I couldn't pretend anymore. If only mirrors wouldn't
glare at me, slowly driving me mad. If only I could have Emily's class,
confidence and ease. Her wit and her strength. If only my mother wasn't
so hard to spend time with. So painful that my fear of losing her stops me
from breathing. If only panic attacks didn't wake me up, cold sweat, my
body waiting to lose something. If only I didn't mistake the need to feel
something besides dull numbness with the need for a relationship. If only
I was more aware of what was happening when it was happening. If only
I could understand, let alone explain, how the best summer of my life could
also be the worst. How the tightest friendship won't talk about one thing.

Sometimes I wish I could say my life changed in a moment. I wish I had
one moment to blame. One moment to hate, replay again and again. "I
have six years and a summer. Six years and a summer changed my life,
sometimes drastic, those were the easier times. Sometimes small changes
that crept up on you and you didn't realise they were hardening
a part of you. I can't hate six years and a summer. I can't blame one

multiplying cell, not just one cell though, but every doctor, every friend's sympathetic look, every family's tears, every bad night, every piece of good from so many people. Pity food tastes awful; you can taste too many different kitchens. Every flower smell mixing together into a sour stench. Every card written creating a terrible play, each uncomfortable second between friends not knowing what to say. Each wonderful moment spent with her, hug, kiss, the taste of her temples, so sweet. Her fear. Her anger. Her love. These are what changed me, changed my life, not a moment. Six years and one summer.

"Blues Tomorrow"
Deirdre Dore

First performed (under the title *Voices*) by the author at The Big Secret Theatre, Calgary, Alberta, as part of One Yellow Rabbit's Summer Lab Intensive.

A baby's attic bedroom, late afternoon, suburbs. Mrs. Vicki Jones, a new young mother with a bad case of postpartum blues. She twists a ragdoll in her hands, speaks to the tiny "angels" in the wall.

MRS. JONES

I see you in the wall, and I listen. I'm smoking, I'm open, I dance. I'm the blonde in the attic with the scar. The young mother who stays indoors. I haven't slept in three days, I haven't eaten in four, and shit… I forgot to name the baby. Gregory Peck was my first choice, I hear that's taken.

I'm clasping, I'm owning, I'm breaking apart, I drank the baby's pee one day. Husband caught me. Now things are changing. Is that his train? His train? Or is that crying?

My mother-in-law is coming for dinner. Husband told me to cook. And name the baby. I made bread pudding which everybody loves and canned peas which everybody hates. Now that's what I call a balanced meal. Don't let me forget to turn the stove off.

So I told my mother-in-law about you. I said I got tiny jumping angels in the gyproc, telling me what to do to my own baby. Yeah. She said she didn't think that was funny. She's coming for dinner, husband told me to cook. I made bread pudding, I killed it myself. I can do that.

Don't let me forget to turn the heat off. And name that baby. I'm cracked across the middle like a rotten egg and my insides are talking back. I've been awake for four days, I haven't eaten in five, I'm zooming, I'm spinning, I'm in exile. The world is delighting in horror.

My mother-in-law is coming for inspection. She brings her own rubber gloves and she wears them. I'm stuttering, I'm shuddering, I'm reeling. Dying is like sleeping only longer. Don't let me forget to turn the bath off.

How do babies get dirty? He's never been outside, not since he was cut out of me. The dirt must be coming from the inside out. Is that the train? Is that the train? Or is that screaming? Don't let me forget to call my doctor.

Mrs. Jones how's it going? How's the baby? Is he sucking, is he feeding, is he growing?

Well he seems a little reckless and I hear voices.

Relax; put your feet up, it's normal.

It's normal, it's normal, oh boy. The thing is I'm afraid. To be alone. With my own baby. Afraid to be alone with my own body. He never had a baby cut out of him. He thinks it's like having a shit. Well it's not.

I don't need no Prozac or Paxil. I got this killer black leather skirt cures depression. Depending on the voices in the wall. Gonna paint you over, blue tomorrow, blue. Tomorrow.

I'm brooding, I'm sulking, I'm bleeding. My mother-in-law is coming to smell the blood. I made blood pudding which everybody loves. I'm boiling, I'm drowning, I'm sticking and it's really hard to find the time to do all that.

I'm lucky. Some women wait their whole lives… for a wee one. They dream for him. And when he comes… they stick pins in his eyes. I'm not making that up.

My mother-in-law is coming for the hearing. She brings her own rubber mask and she wears it. I'm banging, I'm hiding, I'm dying. I'm loving, I'm listening and I'm killing. I drank my baby's blood one day. Man caught me, now things are changing. Don't let me forget to name the baby. Don't let me forget to name… don't let me forget… don't let me. Don't.

from

Housekeeping
Alexandria Haber

Clay is a young widow struggling to cope with the recent death of her husband and being a single parent to a wild little boy.

CLAY

       I locked Evan in the closet yesterday morning. I did it because I didn't want to kill him. It was him or me: one of us had to go. And if I left him to roam around the house while I locked myself in the closet he probably would have chopped his fingers off or broken the television set. I know how horrible it sounds. You think before you are faced with the reality of children, that you will never lose your temper or let them eat candy or watch television. You don't know how they have it in for you from the very beginning. Evan didn't sleep for the first year of his life. I'm not joking. I'm not even exaggerating.

I used to go to a play group with this well-intentioned group of mothers. We would sit in a circle and they would talk about home-schooling and letting their children sleep with them until they were eighteen and nursing them until they were practically old enough to open the fridge and pour themselves a glass of milk. I thought I could be like them at first. I wanted so badly to be a good mother. To raise these organically grown unprocessed freethinking babies. They would sit smiling and calm while I paced back and forth with my screaming son, vaguely comprehending the conversation through my sleep-deprived stupor. I would attempt to listen, as they would offer advice on how to get him to calm down. Hilary, who I always secretly despised ever since she had rejected my homemade banana bread as being too riddled with additives for her children, even went so far as to suggest perhaps I could try calming him down by rocking him in a rocking chair? I said well, yes in fact I had thought of that, in fact I had moved on from that to knocking myself over the head with a rocking chair figuring at least

I could make my head hurt so much I wouldn't notice the piercing shrieks of my son.

I stopped going to play group. What after all was the point? But I wonder now if I should have stuck it out. Because now, now Evan wakes up in the morning and climbs on top of the fridge before I've even poured a cup of coffee. Then he announces he will pee into his porridge from the top of the fridge. And he will.

And he does. And all before I have poured a cup of coffee. And probably somehow it's my fault. I let him eat macaroni and cheese seven days in a row, or I fed him too many hot dogs or let him watch too much television. Maybe it's because I stopped going to play group. Who knows why? Who cares really?

All right. I care. It plagues me. Is it all hit and miss? A game of chance? I mean I know there are some big mistakes. Ones you can't ever stop dreaming about. Like those dreams I had when I was pregnant about having the baby in a basket beside me in a huge stadium and then carelessly leaving and only remembering I even had a baby after I'd walked through hundreds of people and down thousands of stairs. There are unforgivable twists of fate. But I'm not talking about that. What if he grows up to be a ten-year-old who murders a two-year-old or a fourteen-year-old who terrorizes old ladies or a twenty-five-year-old who beats up his girlfriend. What if I miss the signs?

Do I blame it on the processed cheese or his father not being around long enough or me locking him in the closet (please God, not that) or what?

"Karen"
from

Just a Little Fever
Caitlin Hicks

We meet Karen, a commodities trader who is having an affair with a co-worker, one of the biggest traders in the pit. She contemplates an invitation to a lavish party in the home of her lover, Sam.

KAREN

That's me, the one with the crown on my head. My daddy used to call me his little princess. I guess I look like a princess in that picture. I was ten. That's my mother at the piano. She would play for me in the afternoons after school. Once a week, I went to ballet lessons and the rest of the week, except Saturday and Sunday, I would move the furniture, push back the rug and just dance! My mother sat at the bench, humming, and I would get on my pink tights and my slippers and just leap and jump and twirl across the floor! She pretended only to be looking at the music, but now I'm sure she watched me from the corner of her eye. In winter, on Saturdays, we went skating together. In summer, we went on holidays, usually driving somewhere.

On one of those trips, when I was eleven, we were travelling through Texas, and we stopped at a steakhouse by the road. It was this tacky place with stuffed bears and antlered deer and buffalo hanging on the wall, and they had this running bet with anyone who came in the door. If you could eat 32 ounces of steak in less than an hour, your meal was free! But we were too hot for that. I was picking at my meat, and they started arguing, so I plugged up my ears with my fingers. Then, my mother, who was sitting next to me, pushed herself from the table.

Something was wrong, because suddenly she was quiet. I looked up. She had her hands around her neck, and she was trying to talk! To breathe! She looked so surprised! She was panicking at Daddy, fear in her eyes, and hope too. My dad just stood there, with his arms outstretched. I ran to him, he pushed me away, and from the floor I could see her feet stumbling around on the dirty carpet until she fell. All the shoes and legs gathering around, shuffling, hypnotized, in a circle. I crawled to her leg, kissing it, kissing it, kissing it. Trying to save her.

I was just a kid; there was nothing I could do. I kept seeing that look on her face: "Please! Do something! Save me!" It said. And my dad. So lamely reaching across the table like a beggar.

The men can't save us.

"The Wife"
from

Aria
Tomson Highway

Aria is a one-woman show where an actress plays the roles of several different women from all walks of life. The Wife's monologue recounts events in her life, and especially in relation to her husband.

THE WIFE

My husband's socks, my husband's pants, my husband's shirt, my husband's underwear. My shirt, my socks, my pants, my underpants. Hey, the way this life of mine has gone, loving him and him loving me and me and him go fishing in the lake. You throw the net. And the water sticks in the (*hand motions making the shape of the webbing in the net*) catching the sun. Handfuls of light come "phht-phht" in your face. "*Hera Keechigeesik,* don't rock the boat too much. Scare the fish away," he say to me. Me and him. Hey, *ta-p'wee-sa pee-sim*[1]...

The years me and Zachary were fishing and trapping up north, summertime we live in tents. The lake is there, the island, the island hanging from the sky. Our men were all gone hunting. So it was just us women. And the children. Alone.

All of a sudden "haw-woomp." This "phhhrrroommm." Very black. First I thought it was a moose. But no. "Haw-woomp, haw-woomp," the water went, "haw-woomp, haw-woomp, haw-woomp." It was terrible. There was this...*pee-s'tew*[2]... this... foam... foaming in the water. It reached the shore. It was huge. Bigger than any man. Covered with hair. No lips. Eyes flames of ice. It was. The Weetigo! Ohhh, the breath of the Weetigo can freeze you till you're stiff as a statue. Then the Weetigo enters you. Right into your soul. And you become. The Weetigo! And you eat people. Brrrr.

So anyway. There, The Weetigo. On the shore. Right before our very eyes. So us women. We grab our children and take to the hills. And we waited. And I watched.

The Weetigo went into my tent! Rowwwowwwooorrr! (*roars and bangs the sides of the washing machine*) It roared and raged. The tents were in shreds. The dogs? All dead. He was so big he tripped on the stove and burned out camp to the ground. Everything was in flames.

Then. And only then. "Haw-woomp, haw-woomp, haw-woomp, haw-woomp, haw-woomp," it swam back to the island. Brrrr! The Weetigo is a terrible, terrible thing to see.

(*Abruptly, she begins to sing, happy as a lark.*) La-la-la-la-la-la-la the month of high July, hey! (*speaks*) The life of wives sings in the summer the furniture needs dusting, hey! *Ta-p'wee-sa pee-sim nee-ta-cha-ga-soo.* "*Hera Keechigeesik*, that yellow sunshine sure looking good on that brown belly of yours," he say to me. Zachary. My Zachary.

My husband's sock, my husband's pants, my husband's shirt, my husband's under…. The time that Nataways woman brought his underwear home to me. In a box, all nice washed and folded.

She stands there. Curlers. Blouse wrinkled and dirty tits stink of ashtrays and men. One step down on my rickety porch, paint is gone long ago, wood rotten sand blow through the cracks. Jacket, Zachary's pup, the ugly one, dropped his shit by the step again.

That Giselle Nataways. She took a shit on Liza Jane Manitowabi's lawn. She opened her legs to seventeen-year-old Dickie Bird Halked right in front of Black Lady Halked's face. She made two babies by Raggedy Annie Cook's husband without missing one single goddamn bingo game. But no woman come near Zachary Keechigeesik.

I, Zachary Keechigeesik's wife, never let her children go hungry, never missed a payment at Andy Manitowabi's store. I, Zachary Keechigeesik's wife, walked 40 miles to the Anchor Inn in January through that blizzard to sober up Rosie Kakapetum the medicine woman to save this woman's own mother from the blood from that accident, the gun in that drunken brawl this woman's own father was the one that pulled the trigger and just about shot her foot off. I walked that 40 miles.

She stands there. Her lips smile. But her eyes? *Ee-pa-pee-it a-wa k's'ka-na-goos. Ku-nu-wa-pa-ta oos-kee-si-g'wa.*[3] I freeze. I hear rushing water in my head. (*screams uncontrollably*) I kick with my knee. I kick and I kick and I kick and I kick and I kick. (*Pause. Calm again, she whimpers.*) Blood got all over my hands. Blood and clumps of sticky bloody hair. I kicked her in her pregnant belly. Her shitty brown bum spread naked in the dirt by my broken steps, squeaking like a sick mink.

I was ever alone. Three days. I sit in my living room. Curtains shut. Don't eat. Don't wash. Nothing. Three days. Stare straight ahead. Three days.

He come home, shy as a puppy dog, this… suitcase full of dream visions under his arm—the very first TV on the reserve. So. So now me and him and him and me. We lie on this couch at midnight. (*pause*) Can't see the TV too good cuz his knobby old knee's in the way, hey. *Ta-p'wee-sa ma-na a-wa pee-sim.*

[1] *This phrase is used at various times in this monologue, in various permutations. Its approximate meaning, in Cree, is "Hey this sunshine sure feels good…"*

[2] *"Pee-s'tew" means "foam" in Cree.*

[3] *Cree: "She's laughing at me, this female dog. Look at her eyes."*

from

Star Light Star Bright
Janis Rapoport

Estelle is a thirty-six-year-old childless woman who works as an astronomical photographer. Her husband, Lewis, is a thirty-eight-year-old successful surgeon with a sub-specialty in men's genitalia. The time is the 1980s.

ESTELLE

> *Addressing images of stars, single and in clusters, that surround her, dome-like on three sides.*

You are conceived in violence and passionate explosions. Heat… eruption… collapse. Star light, star bright, nurtured in your mother's cloud womb, feeding on swirls of gas. You are hot, hot, hot. Bright in your nursery of dust, you cluster with brothers and sisters, spectacular jewels along your mother's spiralling arms.

To survive, you fuse your core with celestial energy. You struggle, balance, dance. The universe sings to you: open, grow, believe. Another force is whispering: stay, conserve, contract. While you are a juggler, you are alive. But, when you can no longer, you explode in a furious wind, vanish, your radiant birth reversed into deep, dark death.

And I? I am your photographer, your decoder. I am your memory, your lightprint and shadow. You fascinate: my greatest challenge, and my sacred hope.

Star light, star bright…

There was a child, at first just a simple prong of light inside my belly, a belly soon expanding by intervals, curving under the vault of the sky. She was to be called Clara.

And I kept on photographing *you*, silver piercers of night: the Dippers, the Pleiades, Upsilon Andromedae. Until not, not, not arced across my mind towards those who couldn't cry or influence or speak, towards guardians whose babies—whose starlight—were womb dwellers, corpses intrauterine.

That's when Lewis called me all those names, names no husband should ever call a wife. It was all my fault, he said. I was to blame for Clara...

On our honeymoon we went to Israel, to the Dead Sea. We floated, our bodies barely above the water. We swam with starfish who curled their arms in welcome. The air was dense. We could taste the salt. The sand was wet with sparkling. On the way back to the tour bus... the pillar.... Lot's wife, they said. I wanted to know her real name before labelling the photograph. I looked back through memory... the sea... the sand... urging the pillar to voice her secrets.

A child...

In the dark room, after, paper moving beneath the surface of the water, eager for light, for image birth...

Clara...

The white border of a photograph is not our final frontier. Nor is the chasm of space where your brightness stretches and stretches.

Star light, star bright
First star I see tonight...

There was a child. Her name was Clara. I thought Lot's wife would have watched over Clara. Lot's wife, who used to cook for angels. While Clara was taking her final swim through my body, slippery with womb water, doctors and nurses came with their needles, and Lewis with his pills. I was already too drugged to stop him. Then the vortex: dark, spiralling. All night I fought to climb the swirling, millimetre by millimetre.

Finally I folded her newborn limbs into the bone cradle of my arms, her tiny dark curls like miniature starfish curving around my fingers. Her toes were freshly plucked pearls. I placed them around my neck, knowing Clara had travelled through that dark funnel into the precision of your starlight.

Star light, star bright,
First star I see tonight,
I wish I may,
I wish I might...

Clara was wish perfect. Perfect and newborn. Newborn... but not breathing.

"Don't Be Sorry"
from

Motherhood, Madness and the Shape of the Universe
Kim Renders

This monologue exists at the end of a larger monologue that searches for a justification for the creation of a life. Why bring new life into a world that is doomed? Having taken the irreversible leap into parenthood, the speaker wonders whether she has made the greatest mistake of her life.

— ⊚ — ⊚ —

SHE

    My mom did this thing that drove me crazy when I was a kid. Whenever I would be very sorry about something… breaking something, losing something… she'd wag her finger in my face and bark at me… "Don't be sorry! Don't be sorry!!" But I was sorry. I really was. It did, it drove me crazy.

Of course, now I'm the mother. Now it's my kids that come up to me with the broken figurine and their very sorry little faces… and *I'm* the one wagging my finger and barking at them… "Don't be sorry! Don't be sorry!!" I'm sure that they don't understand any more than I did, what the hell that means, "Don't be sorry!" But you just want them to learn, "Don't be sorry! Think first!!!"

Right…. Think first.

I never wanted children. I did not have dreams of motherhood. And here I am. And sometimes when I am crippled with worry over all the horrible things that could happen to my children…. When I look at the world and see what people… what WE are doing to our planet, to each other, to our children… I'm sorry. Sometimes I think that having had Finn and Jill was the biggest mistake I ever made in my life.

(ironically, wryly) All for the want of a better condom!

Well, I was feeling like shit the other day. I had gotten myself all worked up over something and I was mad. I was mad at everyone. Robert, the kids, the world. I don't remember what about. About nothing. I was just mad.

I had made supper... the kids weren't eating it. Robert was in the bedroom getting dressed to go curling. He wasn't eating!

I hadn't washed in three days. I hadn't changed my clothes in seven. Why bother? No one sees me. I don't go anywhere. Too much soap is bad for your skin and changing clothes just makes more laundry. Oh yeah... I was mad!

And I said to the kids... "something or other" about "something or other" and they said, "No! Daddy said it's different!" And I said, "Well what does Daddy know?" And they said, "Well Daddy's the boss!"

Daddy is the boss? Daddy is the boss??? Where the *hell* did they get the idea that Daddy.... That *(deep voice)* Daddy... is the boss?

Because I'm a soft touch, right? I let them get away with everything. I'm just the idiot that folds their laundry, right?

"So..." I asked the kids, "If Daddy is the boss. Then what the F... what... am... I?" And Finn... ah, Finn... sits up in his chair wrapping his little arms around himself and says, "You're the lover! You're the lover!"

(pause, pause... smile) Don't be sorry. Right.

"Soft, Sugary Earth"
from

The Adventures of a Black Girl in Search of God
Djanet Sears

RAINEY

"What do you eat?" What do you eat. Asking me like she's my God damn mother or something—I hate it when they do that. See, she doesn't know that I know she's some second rate, just finished her residency, walk-in clinic, witch-cum-doctor.

"Why, whadda you eat?" That's what I was gonna tell her right to her big ass face. But then she wouldn't write me a prescription and that's why I'd stopped there in the first place seeing as how I couldn't drive anymore— retching cinders and cotton balls all onto my lap and all over the God damn steering wheel. And I'm supposed to meet Michael—and I can do Toronto to Negro Creek in just over an hour if no one's looking—but there I am at Avenue Road and Bloor, getting the third degree just to get some meds, and trying to figure out how I'm going to stay over at Pa's when I can't use his toilet. He used to wash toilets, was a sleeping car porter on Canadian Pacific, for years before anyone would hire him as a lawyer. Says he could wash a toilet bowl so clean you could lick the rim, the thought of which really makes me feel like retching all over again, 'cause I can't hardly look at a toilet bowl anymore, even if it's on TV—'cause of Janie. I can't use any other toilet but my own.

> *She begins to form small mounds of dirt. She takes a Ziploc bag out of her pocket and carefully places the earth in the Ziploc bag. She is methodical.*

"I haven't been eating too well. Chronic lesser curve peptic gastritis," falls quickly out of my mouth. Medicalese for stomach ulcers. 'Cause I've been to med school too and I know, I want her to know that. And I know she hears it 'cause while she's looking down her nose at me, her big ass eyes nearly fall out of her big ass head.

RAINEY takes a morsel of earth and places it delicately on her tongue, savouring it.

I should have told her to prescribe omeprazole or a prostagladin. Better yet, 2g of sucalfate a half-hour before I eat. Instead I say, "I don't eat well."

I don't eat well, I know that. What am I gonna tell her, for Christ's sake? I'm an obstetrician? Haven't practiced in three years? That it started when Janie was still inside me. Me, secretly bingeing on freezer frost from the old fridge we'd bought in Fergus before Martha, my mother who raised me, before Martha passed—I hate that word—"passed." Gone on. Like there's something to go on to. I could tell her the truth, tell her I've been trying to get out here all my life and now, now I just hunger for the soft, sugary earth by Negro Creek. My Pa's family's lived and died on this bush land—been ours since the War of 1812. Maybe that's why it tastes so sweet. My great-grandmother gave her life to this water trying to save a soldier's uniform. Lorraine Johnson. I was named for her.

The water almost re-enacts the scene.

Her grandfather Juma, Juma Moore was granted this Ojibway territory for fighting against the Americans in the Coloured Militia. Once a year his uniform would get a ritual cleaning. They'd go in the water with it, hold it under, and let the creek purify it. Lorraine had done it for years, but this time…. Well, she was in the water when it happened. The uniform slipped down, out of her hands and she went after it. They found her downstream when the creek thawed that spring, her hands still gripping that jacket. The authorities returned her body but kept the uniform—said it was the property of Her Majesty's army. They can be like that sometimes up here in God's country. Christ, they can be like that in the city.

I should have told her, I should have just told her, told her now since Janie, I yearn for chalk to dry the flood inside me and that's why I pop aspirins, only 35 on good days, not just any, it's got to be Bayer, original, not extra-strength or that Life Brand shit, just Bayer acetylsalicylic acid, and, that's why I've got me a hole in my belly—it's white willow bark. Aspirin, it's willow bark. So I've got a tree growing inside me. And I can't take the iron pills I need. Any doctor worth her salt knows that the intentional and compulsive consumption of non-food substances is eradicated with a forceful regimen of iron. But I can't hold something that heavy inside me— falls through the holes in my belly when I swallow and when it stays down, it bungs me up so bad I have to sit on a toilet for days, and I don't like to sit down on toilets, since Janie. Could you just see her face if I told her I was now eating ashes from cigarettes, not that I smoke them or anything, it's just, well, I don't know why, and it's got to be Export A, and I don't know why Export A. I'm just praying.... Funny, I'm praying a lot lately. I don't know why I do that either. I don't even know that I'm praying. Praying for one more aspirin before my guts fold into my spine, or I'm praying to reach the toilet, in my house, before I weep all over the floor. I'm not praying to God though. God, the Father. No father of mine would allow Janie...

> *RAINEY searches out a new section of earth and begins to discard the top layer of dirt with her hands.*

I can still feel her.... Wrapped around me. She would hug me round my waist so tight sometimes like she was trying to get back inside me, like I was her fingers and toes and she'd missed having them around her all day, like I was her everything. She was...

Janie on the toilet—that's all I remember sometimes—that's my only image of her. Janie on the toilet holding my hands. Five and frail with a fever and I can fix her, there's a doctor in the house, Pa's house. And it's late. We'd been running through the woods all afternoon, she loved the woods so much, laughing and yelling for me, and she's got a fever and her neck hurts, but we've been running. And I send Pa with my car to get some Tylenol, Children's Tylenol, and she's on the toilet, so clean she could lick the rim and I'm holding her, holding her on the toilet and, and she, she, she, she.... She falls, falls... on me. And I can't find the keys to Pa's car and I'm running.... Running with her through the middle of Holland Township, wishing I had wings, feeling her slip away from me, going somewhere without me—she always, always, always wanted me to come along with her before.

She's gone. They tell you she's gone. She's in my arms, I'm looking at her and where's she gone. She's in my arms. I see her little copper feet, I see her tiny brazened fingers, her gilded neck, her ferrous freckled skin, her coral lips... I know I'm looking at her. And I know... I know she's not there. And I'm, I'm, I'm... I'm wondering where she went.... And you feel... I feel...

> *RAINEY looks up at the sky.*

Ten billion trillion stars in the universe. Ten billion trillion stars. That's not even counting the planets revolving around them. But it's mostly dark matter. It's 99% empty. One huge vast realm of nothingness. Janie… Janie…

"Janie"
from

The Adventures of a Black Girl in Search of God
Djanet Sears

— ◎ — ◎ —

RAINEY

And I am a doctor, Michael. She had all the symptoms. It was textbook. It was textbook. It's why, it's why…. It's why I…. When Martha got sick… I prayed. I really prayed, Michael. I told him. I told God, bring her out of this please, and I'll do anything. Anything! And when she…. When she dies, I thought… I thought, find…. Find…. You're just going to have to do it yourself. I left the seminary. I had to learn how to help, really help people, heal people…. Cheat…. Cheat death. And when I saw my first birth… I'd studied, I mean, I'd seen the films. When I saw life come into being, come into the room. When I caught the miraculous fruit of life with my own two hands. I knew that's what I wanted to do. Bring life. Help bring as many lives into the world…. Catch as many new souls. That was cheating death. It makes no sense, but that's what I thought. I mean, meningitis is…. If I couldn't catch meningitis in my own child, to save her, save me, and truly do battle with death…. You know…. You know how much I wanted babies, our babies…. And when we kept losing… I kept losing…. Then Janie…. She stayed. She grew. She was…. She would hug me round my waist so tight sometimes like she was trying to get back inside me, like I was her fingers and toes and she'd missed having them around her all day, like I was her everything. She was…

In my mind I'm still there, on the toilet. I'm on my knees in front of her, holding her hands, and she falls…. She falls forward on me, on my breast. She's playing. I thought she was playing. I feel her heart beating so fast. And she won't wake up, Michael. I try, I try to wake her up. She's in my arms. And I'm calling 9-1-1. And then I don't feel it. I don't feel her heart anymore. And I run. I start to run. I'm running. 'Cause it comes to me. If I can just run fast enough, faster than time, time will start to slow down and go backward, and she'll be…. And I can't. I can't run fast enough, Michael. I can't run fast enough.

I… I just…. If, if I start to feel…. If it starts, it's, it's…. If I cross the event—if I cross the horizon, I'll never come back, it's never ever going to stop. I'll drown, I'll drown in it.

"Rebecca"
Dalbir Singh

Cork, Ireland. Rebecca, is a Caucasian woman in her early fifties. She is on the edge of a cliff.

— ⊚ — ⊚ —

BECKA

(with Irish accent) My son, Sam, picked me up after dress rehearsal once to take me out to dinner. And as we walked past the faded red brick of the community theatre, I knew he was going to kill me with some bad news. He didn't talk much, averted my eyes, kept his distance just in case I were to strike out, just in case I were to push him accidentally off a cliff. And I did. I pushed my baby off a cliff that night. That night he told me over smoked salmon and Chilean wine he had fallen. Fallen for a dark, an Indian girl from Dublin. A dark girl from Dublin. And I sat there, with a knife in my hand and a look of death on my face. And I calmly just got up, and walked out of there. He followed me in his car for quite some time, honking, yelling for me to stop, to stop, to stop. But I didn't. I walked for what seemed like miles along the coast, along the ocean, seething, just seething with rage. I was walking on numb legs, I was walking, being carried by rage, absolute rage. Rage, driving me through the streets, past all the dirty gypsy children, rage carrying me through the underbrush, and into my backyard, past the old blue rusty swing set, five metres from the cliff's edge, rage pushing me up the stairs, up the burgundy carpeted stairs, and into Sam's bedroom, grabbing his school trophies, grabbing his middle-school attendance record, grabbing his armless ten-year-old teddy, grabbing his history, throwing it into a box, rage, rage, rage leading me downstairs, through the humid night air to the cliff's edge and rage cradling me as I threw my baby's history, threw him into the sea.

  Pause.

And now on nights like these when the humidity rises up off the sea and clings to my body I feel like drowning myself in sharp ice, I feel another panic attack on its way and every time, right before I slowly sink to the ground and close my eyes, I see your face. Sam, I can see you, feel you coming home. Not lost, never lost. I swear I can smell that cologne, your smell in the hot humid air. I can hear your wet bare feet on the rocks, climbing, climbing back up. And I wonder if this is the night I'll hear your voice, I'll hear you walk through the ripped screen door and call and call and call me.

    Pause.

I can hear you calling me.

from

I Am Yours
Judith Thompson

Hospital. Dee, having left her pre-surgery bed and wandered down the halls, in her gown. She has felt the life of the foetus inside her and cannot go through with the abortion. She now walks towards the audience: she addresses the audience as if it is the foetus.

DEE

A feeling like a push; somebody strong, pushing me off the table, it was not a... decision, I was pushed and I felt and I feel and I hear... a breathing... inside me, that is now my own. I do... hear it. A raspy kind of sweet breathing a—a pulling for breath, for air and a kind of a sigh of content. I feel the breath on my face the drops of wet breath, hear a sigh, are you there? A voice not mine, a voice like no other; there you are, in the sighing, and I know I think I know whose voice this is; this is yours, this is yours, this is not a mirage, no, nor part of the madness, a moment of clear, oh yes, you are clear, I can taste your sweet breath, a flower, not mine, not mine but inside me I can feel on my hand the press of your hand, fingers, holding my hand, tiny fingernails, not letting go, the impression, the feel of a tiny body lying next to mine, breathing, in the bed, cream sheets. You are showing me, showing me, you are looking at me with your dark blue eyes, staring at me in the dark in the night, smelling my milk, breathing fast for my milk, the shininess of your eyes like the moon on the water I see: I see it, too clearly, just as I can hear your voice, too too clear, rising, falling, your eyes, looking at me from across the room, watching me move across the kitchen, watching me; when I hold you and you wrap my hair around your tiny hands, pulling, and your head on my chest rooting for the breast, I can hear, I can feel the rooting. I am lost, I have heard you, I can feel you drinking of me, you drink my milk and you drink and you drink and oh, I am lost.

from

The Monument
Colleen Wagner

Stetko has dug up a mass grave and has removed the corpses of several women and girls. Mejra has discovered the body of her missing daughter and finally tells him about her, lifting her out of the faceless, nameless dead.

MEJRA

Her name is Ana
She was nineteen.
Young-looking for her age.
She wanted to be a teacher—of philosophy.
She respected all religions.
She was brave and kind at once.

She had a thin line of black hair that ran up to her navel.
And watery eyes
like a doe's.

She felt every person had dignity regardless of their race.

She believed love was the answer.
Patience was the teacher.
Compassion was the mirror.
She would say, "I am the reflection of love and trust and joy—all that you are but haven't yet recognised.

You are going to tell the story of the missing ones.
The women and children.
You are going to name them.
We are going to build a monument to the truth about war.
We are going to let the mothers reclaim their daughters.

"I Should've Done It Sooner"
from

Women's Stories
Irene N. Watts

Mary James is a middle-aged battered wife in a women's shelter. She pours out her story to a social worker.

MARY

Now, I can't think why I put up with him for so long. I'd wished him dead so many times, I never had the courage to say anything, but sometimes I'd catch myself talking, whispering when I was alone, "I wish he were dead." Even in my thoughts I couldn't confront him directly, it was always "him", not "you".

In the beginning I read women's magazines: TIPS FOR A BETTER MARRIAGE. IS YOUR MARRIAGE WORKING? Mine wasn't, so I did everything they said: Toys put away, kids ready for bed, my blouse changed, hair combed, put on fresh make-up. His dinner waiting for him, whenever he chose to come home and eat it, a pot of coffee on the stove, freshly brewed. Every day I reminded the kids not to bother their dad when he came home from work. He was always late home, so I ate early with the kids. It was better that way. He didn't want to see my face across the table, "accusing him" he said. I never knew what was going to set him off, a look, a word. One night I made a shepherd's pie. When he was sober, he said it was almost as good as his mother used to make. I was afraid the pie might have dried out in the oven. He was later than usual. I made fresh gravy the minute I heard his key in the door. "Ready in a minute dear, I'm just pouring the gravy over the potatoes the way you like it. You're a bit late tonight." I set the plate down, he picked it up and threw it against the wall, "nagging bitch" he said, and slammed his fist in my face. After I'd cleaned up the blood and gravy, I made him a sandwich. "Sorry, it's only cheese" I said. I was always apologizing, wondering how to be a better wife, how to please him. He started on Beth when she was twelve. Beth is our eldest, the boys are ten and five, his "little men." She came in from basketball practice, her cheeks flushed, her eyes shining. I heard her call out something to her friends. She never asked anyone in, he didn't like it. "Where were you?" He towered over her, pushed his face close to hers. I heard the words he'd said to me a million times, "tell me the truth slut."

When she tried to tell him he hit her across the mouth. I'd just finished making next day's lunches. The bread knife was still in my hand, I threw it at him, it stuck in the side of his neck. He never made a sound, just slumped over. We watched the blood trickle down his shirt collar. I twisted the knife a bit before I pulled it out, then I called the police. That's how easy it was. I should've done it sooner.

she
speaks

PASSION

from

'da Kink in my hair
trey anthony

— ◎ — ◎ —

SHAWNETTE

I got a kink in my hair. You used to love to play with that kink in my hair when it was all sweaty and damp. Kinky hair matted to my face. Sweat and your love dripping between my thighs. My love and me imprinted on your ebony skin, and you tracing my nose with your tongue. You just loving the roundness of my butt, grabbing, chocolate brown skin between your fingers. Kneading me like dough, kneading chocolate dough. *(beat)* Needing me? *(SHAWNETTE looks out into the audience.)* And we sat in that matchbox apartment dreaming about the house on the hills, the Benz in the driveway, the maid getting the door, our kids running around. I said my girl would have a pony and you said my little man gonna take golf lessons or something. *(laughs softly)* And let me tell you I would go to the beauty parlour all day. Get my nails done and do my hair. And you would say do those nails and even them bad feet, but don't get rid of that kink in your hair. And I believed you. *(shakes her head in disbelief)* I believed. I believed you when we didn't have money for the rent. As I swept and scrubbed white women's floors I still believed… I believed in you even when a can of tuna was an appetizer, a three-course meal and a late-night snack I still believed. And you used to say "Baby, pretend it's caviar." And I tasted the caviar. Tasted your hunger. Tasted your thirst. Tasted your need to fill me up. And I became full on your hopes, dreams, full with your desires. *(beat)* Satisfied with you I became full. Unbuckled my belt buckle as my stomach overflowed with you and your wishful food of dreams. And we laughed and dreamed. And we dreamed and laughed. And you played with that kink in my hair. *(beat)* So I got another job so you could go to med school. *(beat)* Left you studying at night as I caught the #5 Downtown Train of Faith, connecting to the #23 Bus of Hope. I cleaned those offices and I dreamed. *(beat)* I ate caviar sandwiches on my ten-minute break. And when I came home all tired and torn you p___. with that kink in my hair. Sweat and your love dripping between my thigh. *(beat)* Filling me up again with you…. So forgive me if I feel to choke now! I got a burning desire to spit you the Fuck out! *(beat)* Because I paid my dues! I did my time! I made you! I loved you! I believed you! *(softer tone and in disbelief)* So I just don't get how she's there and I'm here. *(begins to cry)* I don't get how you got a houseful of beige kids and not my kids! I don't think she remembers tuna/caviar! *(beat)* I don't think she mended your spirit and patched up your soul! *(beat)* She met you! But she never dreamed you! Believed you! *(softly)* She could never dream you… *(Two beats, then SHAWNETTE looks into the distance and delivers the last line with strength.)* And I know there ain't no kink to play with in her blonde hair. *(beat)* You used to love to play with that kink in my hair.

"Shona"
from

Exposure
Maja Ardal

Setting: Nursing home, Salvation Manor, run by an order of nuns.

Character: Shona. A highly efficient nurse, who has dedicated her life to geriatric care. She has pride in her work, but has been sorely tested by the arrival, a year ago, of Roger Beech. He rages against his helplessness, and focuses his sarcastic observations on the nurses.

Roger, seventy-eight, lies in bed, frozen with Parkinson's disease. Shona has just found a stash of sleeping pills in his drawer. He has been collecting the pills for several months. Another patient has been found near death from an overdose. Collections of pills have been found in several patients' rooms. Shona has discovered that Roger is the ringleader of this "suicide club." Despite his Parkinson's disease, he is the most intellectually alert, and hostile, patient on the floor.

SHONA

(*with controlled rage*) Have you forgotten how you never spoke a word when you came in here, and how we got you on the right medication, fixed you up, and got you talking again? All you did was yell and swear at me, but I didn't give a damn. I got you wanting to wake up in the morning.

Then when you began to come to singalong, you'd sit there in your wheelchair staring at us as if we were a bunch of morons. Professor Beech would never lower himself for "Yellow Submarine!" Or, God forbid, bingo games! Muttering all through the game what idiots we were trying to enjoy ourselves. Until you finally played one game and won thirty dollars, eh? I saw you looking like the cat that ate the cream!

Did you know, that I heard every word you screamed in the night, begging for Elsie to come back and save you, that it was me who came in and stroked your head, and pretended *I* was Elsie? And you'd talk to me about the days when you fell in love, and how painful it was when she got sick, and how hard you tried to keep the pain away? And you'd go to sleep thinking Elsie was watching over you. Well, mister, it was just little old me. The stupid nurse, who's trying to make your life worth living, and keep you from lying in your own shit, or falling again and breaking your ribs.

Do you know how *happy* I was when you spat out your first insult at me? Everything I say and do makes you mad, and when you snarl and bite, you start to move again! Your body comes back to life! All I have to do is give you a cheerful "platitude" as you call it, and Bingo! You have a reason to live another day! As long as stupid nurse Shona lets herself be the butt of your anger, stupid nurse Shona is doing her job.

But this isn't just a goddamned *job*, mister! As long as there's a flicker of life in you, I'll break my back to keep it going! I'm not torturing you, like you think. If I don't use *every ounce* of strength I've got in me to give you a reason to live, I might as well give up nursing and go work as a prison guard! No! Don't open your mouth, I'm not finished yet! Helen's down the floor fighting for her life because of this sick little suicide club of yours. How dare you play God! And how can you even think that Salvation Manor would let you or anyone else plan your way out!

Or maybe you *want* us to wipe out every old person who begs to be put out of their misery the minute they feel lonely, or have pain. Why don't we just shut down Salvation Manor, and go around to people's homes on call, with big syringes and a truck, and throw you into some landfill site, and make room for the new human beings, eh?! Only the *healthy* ones of course! It's a lot cheaper for society, isn't it?

You are the biggest test of compassion I have been faced with, but I'm not going to let you win!

from

Fifi
Tony Berto

Terry, Fifi, and Able are drinking at the run-down watering hole where they work. Fifi and Able have both been around the block enough times that they approach casual sex as a blasé, yet competitive sport. The monologue is said with an almost maternal benevolence towards a very naive, young Terry. Immediately previous to it, an attractive man has been seen walking past the hall. While Fifi intends to seem indifferent, it ought to be clear that she has had sex with Brandon.

FIFI

Oh my God, Able look! Not right now! Look in the door of the far room! No, not right now. I'll tell you when... it's just the Joeyest of Joeys. Oh, my! I think I'm in love. Did you see that? Leather jacket, pompadour, *and* biker boots. Terry quick, go in there and see what he's ordering. And see if he's alone... and see if he's...

Don't turn up your nose Able, I have my standards, let's leave it at that. Besides, he had so much more...

Terry, pay no attention to Able. I see you're lost dear, let me tell you about Joeys. You know, that kind of bad boy they had in every class in high school. Took a lot of shop before dropping out. Good-looking, all the right parts working but, you know, you just know he's gonna be bad for you.

Oh you know the type. They'll either steal from you, or cheat on you, or stand you up over and over again. They're just terrible to get involved with but you'll have the most inferno-like sex you've ever had. But no emotions allowed. Because then you'll feel sorry for them and then they'll walk all over you. 'Cause their dad beat them and they left home at fifteen and they live in the back of the gas station where they work.

Or whatever. And of course they drink either Ex, or draft without even asking what's on tap, or rye straight. And they'll pay you with this pocketful of change that has all these little mementos that they carry around. And they go for days without washing but they just look and smell sexier. And they'll always get asked to join a table but their minds are always a million miles away. And they're always fatally wounded by some beautiful girl from the right side of the tracks that they had a tragique relationship with years ago.

You know, these archetypes weren't just made up. Every small town has a Joey until he gets killed in an auto wreck and then a new one replaces him. And in a town this size, with the school and all, there's bound to be a bunch.

Thank God.

Oh not that you'd ever want to get close to one, but who has time to get close to anyone these days? Not when there's such an endless supply needing to be sampled and… reported on. And Joeys are made for just that. Just remember to get out before you get in… to them… if that sort of thing still happens to you.

Of course they're the opposite of a Lance. Lances are everywhere, well not everywhere. I know a few. That guy Brandon down at the Black Hole—he's a Lance. A Lance is kind of like your perfect man. He's tall, handsome, healthy, never smokes, doesn't drink too much and everyone likes him and he likes them. They usually have a great future and get along swimmingly in the world… but they're always, I mean always, tragically flawed. They're either impotent, or have cancer, or have to take care of a retarded baby brother or are going blind. They're real movie-of-the-week fodder. Maybe they only have one testicle or on the darker side, maybe they torture puppies but no one knows.

Now, I don't think having one testicle is tragically flawed, not from a sex point of view, or my point of view—at least from a freak-sex point of view, which has a lot to be said for it itself, but I digress. It's in their *own* eyes that they are flawed and therefore are tormented. Stay clear.

And well, you seem to need to know, but Brandon, well, rumour has it that he has a huge porno collection; been raised on the stuff and apparently can't even get it up with a damsel unless he's looking at photos of… well, wide open beav. Even if he's with the most fabu babe that just might be the answer to all his prayers.

You don't trust my delicate lady-like confirmations of… ear-to-the-ground? Honey, *rumour* has it. Need I say more?

from

Entrepreneuse
Elaine K. Chang

Marty, a woman who could be anywhere from thirty to forty years old, is speaking to a male nurse from a hospital bed. The body to which she has devoted most of her attention, intelligence, money, and dreams is ravaged by cancer and in pain. Her mind, however, has never been more active and acute than during rare moments of lucidity, such as this.

MARTY

(opening her eyes) Eewww! That tray smells worse than me. Make it go away, please Serge please. What do they call that? Lunch? Yeah, fuck me it's lunch.

(As she continues, her eyes follow SERGE and the tray around the bed and out of the room.) I know you say I don't smell, but that's just because you're so sweet that sometimes you lie. Truth is I stink. I wake up, like, once every three days, hungry like the wolf, and Christ, the smell. Turns me off. *Oui, c'est vraiment vrai!* It rises out of me from here and there. *(She gestures weakly and impatiently to her chest.)* Here! Where the great big investments used to be, these empty putrid flaps. Is it gone? Oh thank God. Thank you.

(She smiles.) Hello gorgeous. No, I was awake a little before. I think I saw you looking at me through the glass before you came in. Nobody looks at me in this damn place except you. That Cindi… loo… whoever the hell she is, you know I woke up the last time and she was fiddling with my IV and the line was half-filled with blood? I cried a little and jabbered something and she said I must have pulled the line in my sleep. Didn't look at me once. Like, hello, here are my eyes, you're supposed to make contact with them, bedside manner, hello? And I didn't do nothing to the goddamn line. You know I sleep like the goddamn dead.

man ever looked at me like you do either. And I like it. Like you don't
want a thing from me. Hey, you're in your civvies! What are you doing
here? All right then, make yourself comfortable. But beam me up a little
first.

There was one guy one time who didn't look me in the eye, but like you he
wasn't interested in what was further south. I thought he was a loser, but in
retrospect? Maybe he wasn't that bad. He was polite, very old school, not…
aggressive. That's an understatement. Excellent taste in men's clothing and
hairstyles. He wore black Prada pants and he had a very active vocabulary. I
remember. Pasha. Popinjay. Names he gave to the men who walked by our
table or took seats at the bar. His eyes darting all around, picking out this
or that detail of a guy's outfit or something else and sizing him up in less
than two seconds. Young Paladin. That was a good one. Also starting
with "p." He even spotted a pair of silk socks, which he said the guy had
probably found on such-and-such a street in Hong Kong. I thought that
was kind of impressive. He ordered shakers of Manhattans all night and
paid for them in the end. Brushing away my signs, the universal signs that
I Was the Woman Offering to Pay Her Own Way, without any hassle,
without so much as looking at me. And it was good not to have to say
much because I was tired that day. Around then was when I was starting to
get tired all the time. I sipped my drinks and my eyes joined his in darting
manoeuvres around the restaurant. I avoided the pashas and paladins,
thought I should leave those for him. Off my eyes went, solo flight. That
one's a pilot, maybe? Lawyer Lawyer Lawyer. Accountant. Alpha Geek.
Whoa, now there's one Big Behemoth. That's disgusting. Something like
that really should not be let out of the house. Nobody Nobody Nobody.
And well well well what do we have here? CEO of Some Major
Telecommunications Company, maybe. Definitely hot, whatever he is.
Nice eyes. But he's with somebody. Damn. Why do the best ones always end
up with women like that? She's wearing a sweater with little sheep all over
it. That is so disgusting! Oh well, if his idea of the dream woman is Holly
Hobbie, how can the normal girl compete?

You're not familiar with the Woman's Offer to Pay Her Own Way? You've
probably seen it at a table near you without seeing it, you know? A million
times in restaurants and bars across the nation. She rummages through her
purse, smiling. She extracts her wallet, or her tiny tiny ultrafemme change
thingy, which is better. She widens her eyes and draws her mouth into a
soft, inquisitive little "o." Takes less than fifteen seconds and it gets results.

Nine times out of ten, or even more. And meanwhile you're rating Buddy's responses. Some make a huge, look-at-me, I'm-the-last-of-the-big-time-spenders, deal out of the whole thing. Some squint and stare at the bill for a long time before digging into their pockets. They're hoping you'll step up. It's hard not to sometimes, the suspense can get to you, but a pro rides it out as long as she can.

My personal favourite is when Buddy barely glances at the bill, pulls it toward him, whips his wallet out and plunks down his credit card, looking you evenly in the eye the whole time. And he's smiling at you, the whole time. It's kind of like saying money doesn't really matter and you really do, you know? That's very good. That's foreplay.

The nicest man's wallet I've ever seen had an onyx and platinum money clip attached right to it. I said, "What a nice wallet! Love the clip." And Buddy said, "Yes, it comes in handy." Very classy guy, that Wallet Buddy. Neat and tidy, onyx-and-platinum-clipped, crisp green twenty-dollar bills. They used to call money lettuce, or dough, or bread. If I were a gangster's girlfriend in the 1940s or something, maybe I would have said, "Nice wallet. Love the lettuce, sugar."

Once back in Squamish Uncle Doug took my mom and me to the diner I used to walk past some days on the way home from school. I'd slow down as I walked by, and I'd look in to see what people were eating through the steam that collected at the bottoms of the windows on the cold, wet days. Maybe I learned to shoot my eyes in every direction, take a good look at everything there is to see without moving my head, there and then. This would've been after Leslie Bradshaw—she was a girl who walked part-way home with me sometimes—told me it was rude to stare at people when they were eating. People like Poppin' Fresh Prada Buddy and me: we learn how to want through a window, by checking out what everyone else is having for dinner.

The time Uncle Doug took my mom and me—that was the time I had my first salad. It came in a light fake wooden bowl. I had no idea how it would taste. So I stared at it for a while first. And then I noticed an itty bitty snail, crawling along the edge of a piece of lettuce. He was perfect and glistening with salad dressing, moving very slowly. "What's wrong with the little bugger?" The question was for me, but Mom directed it at Uncle Doug. I don't remember what he said because I was busy wrapping my baby snail up in a piece of lettuce. I slipped him into my pocket and took him home.

I called him Herman. He lived for five days in a plastic ice cream container I washed out for him. I poked holes in the lid so he could breathe. After three days he made it all the way up to the underside of the lid, and he clung there, upside down, not moving. I had to lift the container up over my head if I wanted to make sure he was still there. After a while it dawned on me that he'd moved up there to get away from the lettuce, which was starting to rot. But by then Herman had fallen from the lid and was dead.

Oh yes, she called me Little Bugger. Never Martine. My mother didn't understand it's not a term ordinarily applied to girls. Little bugger, you little bugger, get out of here you little bugger. All with that funny accent of hers, that gurgly raspy voice, like razorblades stuck in her throat. Even when Uncle Doug, who wasn't really my uncle you know, was pummelling her so hard that she called out, she would tell me in the strangly voice to get out of here, you little bugger. She never called out for me. You'd think that Doug would have corrected her about the little bugger business. A so-called native speaker of English. But he didn't, not once in the three years he lived with us.

(She yawns.) Where was I? Anyhow, so those were some more of my salad days in Squamish, when time moved at a snail's pace and so on…. Yup, not bad for a recovery, thank you very much. I'm a friggin' raconteur. Raconteuse? Is that the feminimunimine? Form of the word I mean? Sleepy small-town life, and so on. I climbed walls, clung to ceilings with my fingernails to get away from all of it. Things picked up for me after that. I went to better places, I ate better, I dressed and I slept way better. And now, I guess, this is where I've fallen. You know, over the past few days it's started to hurt my ears when that outer door opens and closes? I think it works a bit like a vacuum seal. Maybe it's supposed to? Is there some major medical reason or something?… Yeah, it hurts a little. It's like I'm vacuum sealed and cut into pieces, and my ears that are disconnected from my head pop when you or anybody opens and shuts the door. Like those pop-up cooking timers they stick in turkeys. I'm getting very sleepy now. You always touch my forehead before you open the door to leave, don't you, Serge? Even when I'm sound asleep? I can tell it's you subconsciously… by the smell of your hair, like mangoes and Molly's Reach after it rains. Mmmm yummy.

Natural Death
Sally Clark

A woman in her seventies, (Pamela) is onstage. Her hair is grey with some parts dyed a flamboyant shade of red. She wears an expensive-looking black pantsuit that was fashionable in the 1970s. It is now too big for her.

PAMELA

   I liked Howard. He was a nice man. If you're going to live with someone for forty-three years, you should pick someone nice. And Howard was nice. I know what you're thinking. "Nice–" the kiss of death. But "nice" can go a long way. "Nice" can take you through forty-three years quite comfortably. *(pause)* Howard was rich, too. Nice and rich. And smart—he was smart. You don't find many smart men who are nice. These days, smart precludes nice, but when I married Howard, you could still find nice and smart. *(pause)* And rich. You're probably thinking—"Oh, but I guess you didn't love him." And it's true. I didn't. I told Howard I didn't love him and he said, "You'll learn to love me." And of course I didn't. How can you learn to love someone?… But we got along. I liked his mother. She was nice, too. And of course, I was faithful. People didn't have affairs when I was young. Well, they did, actually. But not my sort of people. There was a small terror in the back of my mind that in the middle of my happy marriage with Howard, I'd meet some handsome stranger and fall madly in love. Someone exotic. Howard and I belonged to the Gilbert and Sullivan society. I was sure I'd meet my true love there. He would be some dashing Englishman that they brought in for the summer to direct *Pirates*. Or TUTS, Theatre Under the Stars. *Carousel*—the wife-beating Billy to my understanding what's-her-name. Well, one can only dream. It never happened. I never met anyone who remotely interested me.

from

Whylah Falls
George Elliott Clarke

Cora Clemence tells her daughter, Shelley, the "facts of life," as she, the lion-hearted, but fiercely kind matriarch, has known them. This casual kitchen symposium is necessary because Shelley is being courted by X—or Xavier—Zachary, a silver-tongued, "whore-master" of a poet...

Cora's kitchen. Cora is doing Shelley's hair.

CORA

Don't give me nothing to jaw bout, Shelley, and I won't have nothin to holler for! Just sit back, relax and be Black. I'm gonna learn you bout the mens so you can escape the bitter foolishness I've suffered. A little thoughtful can save you trouble.

Shelley, you gotta lie to get a good man. And after you gets him, you gotta be set to hurt him to hold him, so help my chucky! Cos if you don't or won't or can't, you're gonna be stepped on, pushed round, walked out on, beat up on, cheated on, worked like a Black fool, and cast out your own house.

Don't suck your teeth and cut your eyes at me! I be finished in a hot second. But you'll hear this gospel truth so long you, my youngest, eat and sleep in my house. Best cut your sass!

Pack a spare suitcase, one for him. If he proves devilish, it be easier to toss him out that way. Put one change of clothes into it so he can't beg and bug you for nothin!

If he be too quiet, he'll ruminate and feel his bottle more than he will you.

Shut up, Shelley! I ain't finished. As I was sayin, a quiet man will feel his bottle more than he will you. Rum'll be his milk and meat for months. It'll spoil him for anything. Won't be fit to drive his nail no mo. So when he's sleepy drunk smack the long-ass son of a gun in the head, tell him to wake his Black-ass body up, and drive him out. If the fair fool don't come back sober, he don't come back. Am I lyin?

You don't know who you gonna marry till after you marry him! So either pay attention or pay a lawyer. If a man be sweet lookin, a heavy-natured man, always pullin on women, and he takes up with some spinny woman all daddlied up from the cash he's vowed to bring you, just tell him right and down that you ain't his monkey in a dress, and raise particular devil. Don't give him no shakes. And if that don't work, don't waste another Black word, grab yourself a second man.

Shelley, slide me over my rum tumbler. Preachin parches the throat. Sides, ma eyes feel kinda zigzaggy today.

If some woman is grinning at your man, tell her straight: "If it was shit that I had, you'd want some of that too." Make her skedaddle. If her fresh fool follows, take everything he got, and don't give a single Black penny back!

Shelley, life's nothin but guts, muscle, nerve. All you gotta do is stay Black and die.

"A Clean Breast"
David Copelin

Lights dim up on a room in a hospital. Tamara Morgan is large and earthy.

TAMARA

It's in there, growin', slow but sure.
An' fuck me blue, I'm gonna die.

I wanna curse my fuckin' brains out!
But not today.
Today I'm a fuckin' lady.
But inside, I am thoroughly pissed off.
Albert says, "Better to be pissed off than pissed on."
Ha.
That's his way of makin' molehills outa mountains, the way men do.
Fuck him anyway.

Remember high school?
In mine they made us read all kinds a shit we can't use, like that
 Shakespeare play about witches and daggers and guys dressed up
 as trees.
You know the one.
Anyway, Father Tom says there's no such things as witches, the Church
 burnt 'em all at the stake, and out where I come from, there ain't
 a lot a trees anyway.

My grade ten English teacher, Mr. Pootsal—Blinky—he went to university
 with this famous actor.
You know, what's-his-name.
Blinky gets him to visit our little shit-ass town, to perform Shakespa-hear,
 la-di-da.
But I hafta admit, this actor's not too shabby.

Bruce! That's his name, Bruce… something.
He reads from *Hamlet*, the one about the prince who's a serial killer?
The words sound like faggots talkin', but Bruce is hot.
We clap all polite.
Then my boyfriend Steve says, "Do something from *Macbeth*."
Well, you'd a thought that he'd farted in church.
Bruce baby goes pale and whispers that there's a curse on that play.
Didn't Blinky tell us?
And Bruce gives Blinky a look that would fry bacon.
Blinky goes: *(TAMARA blinks rapidly several times.)*
Busted!
Bruce says don't *never* say the title.
Just call it "the Scottish play."
Don't *never* quote from it, especially backstage.
(Right, like any of us was ever gonna *be* backstage.)
Brings disaster, he whispers.
But my Steve don't whisper.
Right out loud, he says, "Bullshit."
And everybody gasps.
And then Steve shouts the magic word: "*Macbeth. Macbeth. Macbeth.*"
Blinky and Bruce look like they're gonna shit a litter a kittens.
I jump up and yell, "Come to my woman's breasts, and take my milk for
        gall, you superstitious dorks!"
I was fifteen, brand new tits, no milk, but a lotta gall.
Then Steve and me run over to his place and fuck, and giggle, and fuck
        some more.
That bastard Blinky called my Mum.
I was *so* grounded!

Guess you don't hafta be backstage after all for that play's curse ta kick in.
I'm a little superstitious myself.

Lose one a these, you can't just jump into bed for fun, gotta have a little
        chat first, find out his or her take on the politics of titties.
Will they kiss the scar?
Will they puke?
You don't want a nasty surprise.

What the hell, really?

My God, losin' a boob ain't nothin' compared to those poor women who
get their clits cut off.
Imagine havin' your gramma hold you down while somebody slices off
your clit so you'll be marriage material.
"It's for yer own good, dear."
No pleasure ever, just pain, pain from screwin', pain from takin' a pee for
God's sake, just because their mums and grandmums did, just
because a their religion.
Fuckin' men invented religion to keep women down.
Father Tom warnin' us about sex.
What a joke.

Two boobs, one boob, no boobs, a dollar.
Who cares if lovers like it or not?
Don't need nor man nor woman for makin' whoopee.
Got a big plastic cock.
Got batteries for the big plastic cock.
Bzzzzz.
Oh, baby!
Plastic love's better than no love at all.

I heard about this woman who had a breast cut off.
True story, I read it on the Internet.
Where her boob used ta be, she had the scar tattooed with a Tibetan
mandala.
She says, "If I can't be whole, I'll be a work of art."
Damn, I hope she's still alive.

And then there's Albert.
I tell him that I gotta lose a boob.
One for sure, maybe both.
Albert says, "Jeez, Tam, that's a bitch and a half," then he adds another shot
a whisky to the beer he's drinkin'.
Doesn't offer *me* one.
Then he says, "A man takes a overnight train, gets a berth in the sleeping
car back when they had berths like in them old movies.
The man's about to go to sleep when he sees this woman.
She's across from him and she's forgot to draw the curtain.
She takes off her hair: it's a wig.
She takes out a eye: it's glass.

She takes off her bra: one boob's fake.
She unscrews her left arm: fake.
She unscrews her right leg: fake.
Then she sees this guy watchin' her.
She says, 'What do you want?'
He says, 'You know what I want. Toss it over here.' "
And Albert laughs his ass off.
What a guy.

What'll they do with my boob after they cut her off?
Maybe they'll toss her up in the air and use her for target practice.
"Shoot the nipple out, win a hunnert dollars!"
Or maybe they'll make her an exhibit in the Museum a Great Tits.
"On permanent loan from the collection a Tammy Morgan."
Last night I dreamed that I came outa the anaesthetic and the surgeon was
      singin' *(She sings.)* "Thanks for the mammary."
I woke up laughin'... then I threw up.
I'm so fuckin' scared.

I'm doin' the soap thing in the shower and I feel it.
Just a little soft blob different from the flesh around it.
Usually when I do the monthly checkup, my nipples get hard and I get
      frisky, but... this time, my stomach's dead empty.
I feel again.
Still there.
I jump outa the shower and phone the clinic soakin' wet.
Appointment.
Doctor feels around my chest like it's the high point a his career.
Biopsy.
Go home and wait for the results.
I can't talk about it.
Albert tells me that joke.
I don't laugh.
He gets mad and takes off on his Harley.
I don't give a shit.
I got troubles a my own.
Phone rings.
Report's back, come on down.
Bad news.
Really bad news.

By the time Albert comes home, I'll be half the woman I was when he…
No!
I'll still be all woman.
Just a little less… balanced.

I'll tell that doctor, "Gimme my boob in a doggie bag, I'm takin' it home."
I'll put it in a jar, fill the jar with whisky, wrap it up in "Hello Kitty" paper,
    a present for Albert.
Watch his face when he unwraps it.
If he ever comes back.

If he don't, I got it all planned out.
I'll get me a shirt with velcro instead a buttons.
Paint an open eye around the good boob, and long curly lashes on the scar.
Put on the shirt and hit the sleaziest bar in town.
Order a draft.
Turn around, back to the bar, facin' the house.
Pull the shirt wide open.
"Hey, dudes, here's winkin' at ya."
See who pays for the beer.

I wonder where Steve is now?
Steve, my first, way back when.
He loved this boob.
It was his favourite before it was mine.
The first time, sweet fifteen, on that old blanket, his hand, my tit, that's my
    idea of a living bra.
I loved him so much.
After we run away from class that day, we're in his bed, he says, "Tamara
    and Tamara and Tamara," and I laugh so hard his cum runs onta
    the sheets and dries all crusty.
Later that week, his Mum does his laundry.
She snitches to his Dad, his Dad beats him up again, bad this time, and
    Steve takes off for parts unknown.
Without me.

Everythin' and everybody dies, even Jesus died.
I want to be the only one who never!
Oh, shut up, Tammy, stop whinin'.
Tammy Morgan, the Blabbermouth a Death…
Steve's prob'ly three hundred pounds by now, wherever the hell he is.

Albert's history; they're all history.
(singing) "I will survive, hey hey."
Maybe.
Tamara, and Tamara, and Tamara, lie down on the table.
Take a deep breath, go to sleep.
The masked man says, "Scalpel, please."
And just like that, now ya see me, now ya don't.

Slow fade to black.

from

West Edmonton Mall
Patti Flather

Christine has arrived at West Edmonton Mall. She did it! She drove all the way from Whitehorse in their old truck in snowy February weather, with boyfriend Michael (who has a head injury from a fight) in the passenger seat. She's about to turn thirty, and trying to get pregnant in the Polynesian Room at the Fantasyland Hotel.

CHRISTINE

      Just before midnight we check into the Fantasyland. I love saying that. Fantasyland. I really do. Do you have the Polynesian? The ceiling is clouds and blue sky. The walls have tropical paintings on them. A fountain spurts water from this weird brown volcano right into the hot tub. It's... beautiful. Of course it is. I drove eleven-hundred miles. I only stayed in a motel once before. This is gorgeous. It's fantasy, right?

Yeah. Michael bounces on the waterbed. Oh, I mean, the warrior catamaran with a sail. "We shoulda got the igloo, Chris."

Omigosh, it's five after twelve. I'm thirty now. Thirty years old in the Polynesian Room in the Fantasyland Hotel. It's tropical, it's wow. Glamour. You can't find that in Whitehorse or Prince George or anywhere in between. I mean, tropical paintings. Clouds and blue sky. A warrior catamaran. Indoors. Vancouver's prob'ly raining. My boobs aren't that saggy yet. "Michael I'm thirty now!"

"Old bag. Let's try out this waterbed."

"You're such a kid."

"Yeah." He gives me a kiss. "Happy birthday."

"Michael?"

"Yeah?"

"I love you."

"I know." He giggles.

"Do you…. Um, love…?"

"You women, always wanting to talk."

"But Michael I just need to know this once…" *(beat)*

He says "Sssssh." That's all he says. *(beat)*. Um. *(beat)*.

After we, you know, make love… I don't usually talk like this. I don't even know you!… And then we go in the hot tub which is sooo decadent… Michael goes off to sleep. I'm lying there next to him, I'm thirty years old in the Polynesian Room at the Fantasyland Hotel in West Edmonton Mall, Alberta, Canada, the world, the universe. And maybe finally I hope I'm pregnant. It's the right time. I checked. *(beat)*

The vibrating. It starts down here and RUSHES me full body-check into the boards. Fills me up buzzing big inflatable dolphin Howard me zinging out of my skin. Supersize vacuum cleaner. The mall the room the drive the baby, oh no way can I sleep! I'm here. I'm thirty. I'm, maybe there's this cell meeting this other cell inside me. There's zapping here here here. I can't describe it—electric hot racing. I have to get out of bed now, get my jammies off. Get dressed. Get out. I have to right now I'm sorry Michael. Have to race fly leap through the air with the dolphins. Howard I'm coming!

Hotels restaurants shopping The Oilers. Shops and stores, look in the windows ohh so many. Press my nose against the glass, make it real. World Waterpark. Ice Palace. Deep Sea Adventure. Howard the dolphin. Sea Life Cavern. One two three four five six seven eight nine ten eleven twelve thirteen restaurants bars and lounges on Bourbon Street. The flavour of New Orleans. "Peach cider please. It's my birthday." A casino. It's all around wrapping me up. Big long warm high indoors. Faster Chris hurry breathe it in. Vacuum touch feel. Ohhh.

from

The Malaysia Hotel
Laurie Fyffe

Molyka is a young girl, age twenty. She is Cambodian. Only ten years old when the Khmer Rouge invaded Phnom Penh, Molyka lived out the Cambodian revolution/genocide in various work camps in the countryside. Finally, smuggled to Thailand, she was forced into prostitution in Bangkok's red light district, where she met Kris, a Canadian teacher of English as a Second Language.

This speech occurs the night before Kris is due to leave Bangkok. Molyka has a plan for Kris to assist her in illegally immigrating to Canada. Kris refuses. She advises Molyka, for both their sakes, to give up any such plan.

Note: Yu'en—the Vietnamese.

MOLYKA

I can never give up. I have seen too many things change. A little girl is playing hopscotch in front of her house in the city. She is happy, because she knows nothing. Then trucks full of screaming young boys in black pajamas and red headscarves roar down her street. *Leave the city*, they scream, *everyone must leave the city! The Americans are going to bomb us! Leave Phnom Penh so we can clean it.* Clean it? Why would you clean a city so somebody could drop bombs? What they tell us is crazy but they are waving guns and they shoot people who ask questions, so we do what they say. For four years we do what they say. And now you think your life in the camps will never end, that you will never again feel clean, or get rid of the lice in your hair. All you think of is food; all you do is work. But one night your camp is attacked. The Yu'en have arrived, and this time the screaming young men are dressed in green and suddenly no one is Khmer Rouge anymore. But now you know that any life—any world—can be swept away and another put in its place. All you must do is wait, and watch carefully for the signs, signs that tell you now, this is the moment, if you move quickly, if you jump, you will live.

And that is what you are to me Kris, my chance to jump to a new world.

When I first met you in Pat Pong I think, who is this crazy western girl? What does she want here in this Wedding Brothel? Is she here to pick up men? But no, I don't think you even like men. So, is she here to have sex with girls? Some western women do that. But when I sit with you, you only want to talk. So I tell you my stories. And you listen. You listen like the ocean that swallows everything. And now I know why. You betray me, Kris. You use me; you steal my life like you buy a souvenir. I watch you write it down. Tell me; if you did not meet me, could you write this book?

"Bella"
from

Walking to Russia
Jonathan Garfinkel

In a flashback sequence, Bella tells her daughter Masha about what it was like to grow up in Korets, Russia.

BELLA

We did everything together. Climbing the bales of hay, swimming in the river…. One night a Jewish boy knifed a Pole at a dance. The next day there was a mob in front of the courthouse. I was fourteen and Max was sixteen, we hid in the forest and he read me Pushkin, and I read him poems I wrote.

By the late afternoon we could see flames in the Jewish quarter. We ran deeper into the forest. We picked mushrooms to eat, but instead we threw them at each other. Then we wrestled, and there was this moment I was on top and…. We kept walking without even thinking where we were going. At dusk we found ourselves on a road. We were lost, there was no village in sight. Then we heard a voice, as beautiful as any bird. The trees and fields were swallowed by the night, and the song became more beautiful. We sat on a stone and we were at the Met in New York, me in my emerald sequin dress, him in a tuxedo. And we listened…. The song kept on singing. And when he kissed me, it was as though his lips came from the song itself. *(pause)* We lay together in the tall grass, and fell asleep with the moon in our arms…. But we end up in these prisons, all of us, no matter what we do, we're doomed to ourselves. Oh my God, Masha. Oh God.

"We Are Approaching Our Destination"
Todd Harrop

Indoor parking level of ocean ferry—1990s—Marianne (late teens to early twenties).

An announcement over the PA system alerts passengers to prepare to disembark the ferry. People enter cars, unlock bicycles, etc. Marianne is nearest the exit with her sturdy bike, in clip-on shoes, riding shorts, gloves, helmet—full armour. She tells us why she's travelling.

MARIANNE

I can't tell if I'm seasick or nervous. There's nothing to do on this ferry but walk in circles and rehearse what to say. It would help to know if they're still together. She hasn't written for a few weeks. She started as my camp counsellor but by the end of the summer we were close friends, maybe more. I can't let this one go.

Happened on Talent Night: she sang while looking at me. I felt everyone's eyes, including her girlfriend's. (She was visiting that weekend—sitting somewhere behind me?) It was a song for two women, and I felt like I was singing along, our secret duet. Actually I don't know if she can sing—everybody was lip-syncing—but I do know she loves to hike.

We walked in the rain a lot this summer, together. I can't stand the rain—because of my glasses: can't see without them; can't see when they're wet. The last time we walked together was after Talent Night—I remember she wore a baggy, green sweatshirt, and for once there was mist instead of rain.

We stayed out late—the cold seeped into my bones but I couldn't pull myself away. She was describing her family's cottage when a mosquito landed on her shoulder. I waited and waited to see her reaction when it pricked her, but then I swatted it, slapped her hard on the back and left my hand there, feeling her muscles go tense. She stopped talking but didn't look at me or move away either.

After a while she said, "Do you want some fudge?"

We hiked to her cabin and she took my hand! I remember the cuff of her sweatshirt was damp. I couldn't see the dirt path and I had a flashlight but I trusted her footing and never turned it on. Besides, I was catching wafts of her shampoo and I became an animal tracking her scent.

She slept in a renovated, trappers' hut, some shack once used for skinning hides. When she grabbed a flashlight from her dresser and flicked it on I saw roses lying there, wilted, still wrapped in paper. Her girlfriend had brought flowers and candy. I wanted to turn on my light too but was afraid of what I might read in her face. It wasn't romantic like candles but it was kind'a neat, her beam of light slicing the air as I shivered and looked at the fudge by the mirror.

She peeled off her sweatshirt. Her bra was pale violet satin. The colour surprised me and I liked it. She put on a black sweater—I could smell butter and sugar—then she pecked me on the cheek and said Goodnight!

(pause) So I left, back to my cabin, floating because I saw her when she was vulnerable, and knew she loved me because she cared.

For the rest of the summer we pretended nothing happened—once in a while she gave me that special look and I knew our souls were still joined. When the buses came in September everyone exchanged addresses "to keep in touch!" All I needed was *hers*. I wrote a letter; she wrote back, said she got a new job and was moving. Luckily I managed to track her down: she's now living on Vancouver Island!

Which is where the ferry's docking. I'm glad I'm not driving! A few hours of hard pedalling will calm me down. I just want to talk about us. Wish me luck—no, luck has nothing to do with it. We're soulmates: this is meant to happen, right?

from

Amnesty
Ann Lambert

Sophie Wiseman speaks to a group of aspiring writers at a community college in Montreal.

SOPHIE

When I look back on it now, I think that it is a most remarkable thing that I travelled to a very remote place in Honduras—do you even *know* where that is ?

To write a play. I mean, to find material for a play that I wanted to write about the tragedy of civil war in El Salvador and the plight of their refugees. I didn't feel that I could write about something I felt so powerfully about—without going there to witness, to see, to smell, to hear. I wanted to really understand for myself what these people had lived, endured, survived. Then I would tell their stories.

I would *bear witness.*

And that was their greatest need. *Please tell Canada.* Please tell what has happened to us. Their hopefulness was heartbreaking. It was like Canada was a person—a person who had any influence, any power, any means to change one minute of their experience. *I will tell Canada. I will. I promise.* And they would touch my hair. And follow me everywhere I went. Especially the children. They followed me when I visited the bakery, the shoemaker, the little school… even to the toilets, which were wooden seats over holes in concrete cubicles. They were quite fancy really, given the surroundings… but there were no doors. So when I had to go, (and believe me, I did about 100 times a day) the children would follow me. They didn't watch me exactly. But they would wait patiently for me to finish.

I wiped my ass with old issues of *Cosmopolitan* and Salvadoran tabloids and at least a dozen kids waited for me, maybe amazed that gringos shit and wipe their asses, too.

Anyway. I didn't start this story to tell you about wiping my ass in Honduras.

Did I mention that I was frightened all the time?

I am afraid of guns. And there are guns everywhere. Not in the camp, but all around it. Soldiers—boy soldiers, carry machine guns that are too big for them.

At the first checkpoint into the camp, was a boy—and he put the tip of his AK-47 under my hair, and lifted it off my neck. He said something in Spanish I didn't understand. My interpreter, the most relaxed man I have ever met, also laughed, and also said something I didn't understand. The boy let my hair go. (*beat*)

I will never again travel to a place where children carry guns, and I don't speak the language.

Now it was time to hear their stories, what had happened to them. To do what I had come there to do. We sat at a long table, on a dirt floor in one of the volunteers' huts. The children were outside, peeking through the wooden slats in the walls. Listening. There were about six women. They started to talk, one at a time—in a monotone—in voices devoid of expression.

My husband. My companero. My son. My mother. My brother. My baby.

And the babies with guns were circling the camp.

So I heard their stories. And they were as horrible, as unthinkable as you might… think. They poured out their stories but in that same monotone, like they had done this too many times before to an earnest Canada with good intentions. But then, one woman started to speak quietly, so quietly, I had to lean very close to hear her, and she described what they did to her husband. He had refused to tell the boys with guns where the guerrillas had gone. But actually, the guerrillas had never arrived. It didn't matter. It never matters. They cut off his testicles and his penis, stuck them in his mouth, and left his body by the church door. The priests were long gone.

My son? He was a freedom fighter, home on leave. He was wearing the brand new boots he'd taken off an army recruit, another boy they'd kidnapped off the streets of San Salvador and forced into service. They caught my son and they cut his feet off. They left his feet in the main square in our town. His feet, in their new boots.

I felt I couldn't take anymore. *My son. My brother. My sister. My mother.* They did this to them. They did that to them. *(beat)* I was sitting across the table from my interpreter, my fluent, brave interpreter... and my... foot found his. And we played the most—We played footsie. I wanted his foot. It was all I could touch. We were sitting across from each other at that long table, and my foot kissed his. His foot kissed mine. My foot wanted him so badly, and so did his. If we could have, we would have leaped across the table, pushed everyone away, and had sex right there. I had never wanted someone so badly as that man, on that day.

Never.

When I got home, I wrote their stories. I made art from their misery. But I couldn't set my play in Honduras. I set it in a restaurant in New York, and told the story of a waitress who has waited all her life for... life. She has a brief affair with the Salvadoran dishwasher. There are tragic consequences.

Please tell Canada. My brother. My son. My daughter. My mother. My baby.

And so. I wrote a play.

"*Mary*"
from

Mary's Wedding
Stephen Massicotte

Mary has recently made the crossing from England to live with the colonists, as her mother puts it, in the wilds of the Canada. Tonight, while taking shelter from a prairie thunderstorm, she's met a boy in a barn; a farm boy named Charlie, who's afraid of the thunder and lightning. She helps him survive it by holding his hands and counting the thousands from the flash to the rumble. When the storm passes something about the way his fear and vulnerability changes to confidence and strength makes her put aside her fear of horses and accept a ride home...

MARY

     The long blades of grass blend together and blur. The fence posts smudge as they rise up and by. One, two, three four five-six. A bird flashes across our path. His wings flicker three times and he pushes himself, flicker three times and we're gone by him.

The evening air has turned to wind as our horse's hooves drum out and splash through puddles in the road. Charlie's horse breathes as she runs. In out, in out, shh ha, shh ha, shh ha. Our hooves thunder and pound and splash, thunder and splash right onto the hollow wood of the bridge. The bridge goes by with a deep brown rumble. Then splash on the other side. Shh ha, shh ha, shh ha.

I think it is fear that I am feeling. At least, I think it's fear; the speed, the noise. Breathing and thundering, with this boy that was terrified and hiding one moment and fearless and flying with me the next. Fearless and flying with me, body to body beside him.

And when I finally know that what I'm feeling is not fear but something new... when I finally have an idea that what I am feeling is something entirely different... Charlie is gone. And I am walking up the thirty wet stones and my heart is still breathing and thundering as fast as a charge. And my feet, my feet carrying me as slowly as a snail.

That night, I dream only of Charlie. I hear church bells. I dream of white dresses, flowers and little babies and Charlie is there for all of it. I see him with horses. I see him running with them, riding, in fields, in forests, in evenings and in mornings. I see him riding and smiling down to the sea.

I see him on an ocean liner. I am watching him sail away. The war is on and the Canadians are sailing for England, then France and before long the heart of Germany.

"Love Bites"
Celia McBride

This monologue came out of an exercise during a Master Class with Judith Thompson at Playwrights' Workshop Montreal in April 2000.

CHAMOMILE

We used to fuck when we were drunk. It was the only time he could let himself love me. When he was pissed. Then he'd ignore me. Act like nothing happened. It would crush me. End me. But I would not give up. I thought what we had was real. I believed that the intensity of our fucking came from love. But it came from booze. Booze was our undoing. It gave us permission to touch. We got pissed at the bar one night. Stumbled back to the apartment. We were living together. As "roommates." We couldn't keep our hands away. We couldn't pretend anymore. There was no bed in the place. No furniture at all. We spread these old blankets down and drove into each other, devouring and grasping limbs and pressing for closeness. It was drunk fucking. Not quite working yet insatiable appetites kept us trying. It was never enough. He bit me. Hard. I gasped. Not from pleasure. It was pain. Being numb from the booze I bore it. Because I had him. He was mine. One more time he was mine. He said my name. Moaned it. Somehow I didn't buy it. He was an actor. His intention was sincerity. It rang false. We twisted ourselves into another position. He bit me again. I screamed in silence. Afraid he would stop. It was excruciating. It was torture. I took it. For him. His lips on my skin, his mouth coming open, his teeth sinking in, his jaw closing down. Hard as hard as he could. I punched him. Beat my fist against his back. He wouldn't stop and I couldn't stop him. We quit eventually. We'd been at it for hours. He went to another room. I passed out on the blankets. Blankets on carpet on concrete. Concrete as cold as the ground outside. It was winter. It was Alberta. It was fucking freezing. I shivered all night. When I awoke I went to the bathroom. I sat on the toilet and peed. I looked down at my naked body.

I was covered in them. They were everywhere. Bite marks. Purple and black and shaped like crescent moons. He'd broken the skin. Little red cuts. The curves of his teeth. I touched one. I sucked in my breath. No booze in me now to kill that pain. Holy shit. "I'm covered in bites," I told him. "Sorry about that." Sheepish shame. I kept finding them. I'd discover a new one on my inner thigh or in the flesh of my side. I'd feel the fabric of my clothes come in contact with the broken tissue. I'd watch them transform as the days passed. The darkest blood colours changed to bright yellows and browns. I watched them fade and disappear. Like he did. Those bites were my secret. They were my pride. I loved them. Because they'd come from him. Because I'd withstood them, allowed them to happen. Tender. Painful. Reminders.

"Molly Dushane"
from

All Other Destinations are Cancelled
Colleen Murphy

Molly Dushane, age 55 to 65, is an alcoholic who is urging her daughter, Micheline, to leave the small town where they live.

—  —

MOLLY

Stay here much longer, Micheline, and you'll end up like me— married to a man who was dead for twenty years before he had the sense to slam into a moose! Or end up like Lizzie and she'll end up like Alf Thompson, Ivy's husband. Oh, Alf was one for order and cleanliness. He could smell a picture hanging crooked four blocks away. He'd be in the middle of a hand of bridge and if he spotted a piece of fuzz on the carpet he'd stop the game and SWOOP it up! Poor Ivy, it must have been like living with a vacuum cleaner that was always on. One morning Alf went into the bathroom and locked the door. He started in with the toothpaste and shaving cream, splattered them all over the walls, smashed the medicine cabinet to smithereens—by the time the police arrived and broke down the door poor Alf was pulling the bathtub right out of the floor with his bare hands! So stay if you want. Sit here and watch the buses pull in and pull out but you're never on them. Someday a quiet decent man will come along and take you home and you'll go with him cause it's safe. After awhile you'll hardly notice him pull in and pull out because you'll hardly notice yourself. You'll just pick up socks and more socks, and those feelings that well up inside you, well hell, push them down, play another hand of bridge, watch yourself get smaller like the town, and small towns just get smaller. And never mind your four-leaf clovers, your crosses or your bones—you can hang onto them until your fingers fall off and so what—you're safe because you want to be. Until you meet someone, someone who takes you by the soul and you jump, but you've been safe so long you don't have the guts to face it. "Don't want to hurt him he's too… good, don't want to hurt her she's just a baby…." Once a year in the back seat of a car and that'll give you the guts to tolerate another fifty weeks. Then you get brave, desperate, brave. You think no one's home, so you start taking stupid chances. One afternoon everything collapses into a heap around you and everyone gets hurt, but you're so gutless all you can do is stand and watch. Frozen to the spot—standing, watching. But you'll pay, and your children will pay. Frozen to the spot until you can't get your lips out from behind a bottle long enough to say... I'm sorry Micheline, you paid. You're all paid up.

"Bob"
from

Doc
Sharon Pollock

Bob, the wife of a celebrated doctor, in a downward alcoholic spiral attacks Doc with her version of their life together.

BOB

You don't even see me. You look at me and there's nobody there. You don't see anybody but those stupid stupid people who think you're God. You're not God!

Catherine and Katie are together and BOB moves towards them. BOB grabs Catherine's hand.

And it's so funny… do you know what he's done, do you know?… If I…. If I go into the liquor store, do you know what happens? They say… sorry, but the Doc says *no*. He says… they're not to… and they don't. They don't. He tells them don't sell it to her the Doc says don't do that and they don't. But what's so funny is… every drunk in the city goes into that office on Saturday and they say… "Jeez Chris Doc, spend the whole cheque on booze, the old lady's gonna kill me," and he gives them money…. Gives *them* money.

Katie moves away. Catherine turns her head away as BOB advances on Ev.

Well I don't care if you want to know or not—I'm gonna tell you. I put the clothes out, put that suit out for the cleaners and I went through his pockets, and do you know what I found, do you know? It was something he didn't need for me, something he wouldn't use with me, because I can't have any more, no, I've been fixed like the goddamn cat or the dog so what the hell did you have it for?

from

Harlem Duet
Djanet Sears

— ⊚ — ⊚ —

BILLIE

I thought I saw them once, you know—on the subway. I had to renew my prescription. And I spot them—him and her. My chest is pounding. My legs can't move. From the back, I see the sharp barber's line, separating his tightly coiled hair from the nape of the skin at the back of his neck. His skin is soft there... and I have to kick away the memory nudging its way into my brain. My lips on his neck, gently... holding him.... Here, before me—his woman—all blonde hair and blonde legs. Her weight against his chest. His arm around her shoulders, his thumb resting on the gold of her hair. He's proud. You can see he's proud. He isn't just any Negro. He's special. That's why she's with him. And she... she... she flaunts. Yes, she flaunts. They are before. I am behind, stuck there on the platform. My tongue is pushing hard against the roof of my mouth... trying to hold up my brain, or something. 'Cause my brain threatens to fall. Fall down through the roof of my mouth, and be swallowed up. Slowly, slowly, I press forward, toward them. I'm not aiming for them though. I'm aiming with them in mind. I'm aiming for beyond the yellow line, into the tracks. The tunnel all three of us will fall into can be no worse than the one I'm trapped in now. I walk—no, well hover really. I'm walking on air. I feel sure of myself for the first time in weeks. Only to be cut off by a tall grey man in a grey uniform, who isn't looking where he's going, or maybe I'm not— Maybe he knew my aim. He looks at me. I think he looks at me. He brushes past. Then a sound emanating from... from... from my uterus, slips out of my mouth, shatters the spell. They turn their heads—the couple. They see me. It isn't even him.

from

The Retreat
Jason Sherman

At a writers' retreat, Rachel, an aspiring screenwriter who's been having an affair with her teacher, discovers that she's the latest in a string of conquests.

RACHEL

It's different. You find someone else, someone younger, always someone else, and it won't matter to you, because you're always looking, always leaving, always running away. You'll leave me alone and what'll I have? Nothing. And I'll try to fall asleep and wake up each morning with this one inconsolable fact: I have been left behind. I wasn't good enough. I wasn't good enough for *him*. I wasn't beautiful enough, wasn't dutiful enough. That's it, isn't it? That's the magic formula. Yes, you want me at your side at *screenings* and at *faculty parties*, you want me to stand on the other side of the room while men ogle so you can feel powerful. Then your eye'll shift and you'll see someone else, someone else who'll make you feel *alive*, David. Is that what you need? Someone who'll make you feel alive? Well there'll always be someone, David. Someone to make you feel alive for a day, a week, a month, 'til you get bored and then what? Someone else, always someone else. I don't want that. And I don't want to be the one who lets you do that to someone else. You go back to your wife. I know men like you. You need a great love. You have it, she's sitting there by the phone and your children are asleep and they need... you prick... you've got something the rest of us spend our whole lives wishing for, and you're willing to give it up for what, for nothing.

Index by Author

Index by Title